Passed Down
from mom

A Collection of Inspiring Stories
About Moms & Motherhood

THE UNAPOLOGETIC VOICE HOUSE

Passed Down From Mom: *A Collection of Inspiring Stories About Moms & Motherhood*

ISBN: 978-1-734569-32-2

Library of Congress Control Number: 2020905003

Cover Design: Whitney Mullings, whitneymullings.com

Interior Layout & Formatting: Ronda Taylor, heartworkpublishing.com

The
Unapologetic
Voice

The Unapologetic Voice House
Scottsdale, Arizona
www.theunapologeticvoicehouse.com

June, 2020

Dedicated to all the moms around the world.
Thank you for the lessons.

And a special thank you to all the moms
who participated in this book.

Dear Mara,

thank you for
sharing your motherhood
journey, and for
supporting me in mine.

Love, Vind.

Contents

An Introduction by Carrie Severson vii

Birthing from The Heart: Finding Love Through
Acceptance by Alison Rand 1

A Love Letter To My Daughter by Brita Moe. 11

Twinkle Twinkle, You Are Loved by Pauline Erickson . . . 17

All Little Ants Need Their Mother by Valerie Nifora 25

Creando Una Casa (Creating a Home) by Nancy Brooker . 33

Share by Cori Edwards 45

Learning How to Enjoy Life by Michael Berg 53

Motherhood Awakens Divine Power, Intuition and
Consciousness by Whitney Mullings 61

You're Worthy of Everything You Ever Dreamed of
by Cara Wray. 69

From India to Canada: An Intergenerational Journey
of Courage, Action, and Meaning by Vindy Teja 77

Being a Mom by Holly Hammerquist. 87

The Great Legacy of Marriage and Motherhood
    by Tara Severson. 95

My Mother Delilah Tentis Keenan by Teresa Severson . . 105

Color Me Beautiful by Rachel Dumke 109

Together Apart by Nilda Campuzano. 121

Don't Marry a Mexican by Linda Rubio 129

Conclusion 137

An Introduction by Carrie Severson

M Y JOURNEY TO MOTHERHOOD IS DIFFERENT. MY HUS-
band is a father to three boys. Stepping into a stepmom
role has been the biggest learning curve of my life. Whether
my husband and I have a child of our own is still undecided.
We have only been married for a few weeks at this point. Ask
me again in six months.

What I do know for sure is that motherhood is a sisterhood
all on its own. We share lessons and experiences with each
other in line at the coffee shop, in the lobby of the daycare,
online, and through text messages.

When my husband and I got engaged, I decided to create this
anthology as a way to celebrate motherhood through stories.

Some of these stories are written as love notes to children.
Some of these stories are written as anthems to other moms.
Most are written about lessons learned during childhood.

Regardless of when this book finds you, I hope you enjoy
these stories. I hope you relate to a few of them. Most of all
though, I hope you celebrate motherhood every day from this
point forward.

It's a journey. And one I appreciate. As do the moms in this book.
Carrie Severson, Publisher
The Unapologetic Voice House

Birthing from The Heart: Finding Love Through Acceptance

by Alison Rand

THE ROOM IS QUIET. I CAN HEAR MY HEART BEATING FAST. I am shaking and cold and staring at the bare walls, my hands are sweaty. I can hear the administrators talking to one another, but they are speaking Chinese so I can't understand a word of what they're saying. I am anxious and yet I am so excited.

"Soon, I will be a mother," I say to myself. I have been waiting for this moment for a long time, and it is almost here.

I have never been pregnant or felt the heartbeat of my child inside me. I have never felt my baby kicking inside me or pushed through labor. I became a mother through adoption. I say, "I birthed my children from my heart."

The story of our family would start without having all the questions answered. I was saying yes to many unknowns. I was stretching myself in many ways that I have never been stretched before. I was trusting in a process over which I had very little control. One thing I wasn't expecting to happen through the

1

process of adoption was to find a deeper love and acceptance of myself and my child(ren). I focus on showing love daily and making sure that my children know and feel accepted for who they are and, most importantly, that they feel loved.

When I heard my child first cry, my heart stopped. I could hear the cries coming from down the hallway, and I wondered what to expect when we would look at each other for the first time. My journey to becoming a mother may look a little different, but I am sure I was in labor at that moment. I could feel my heart expand as I waited for the moment when I would meet my daughter.

Prior to deciding on adoption, I thought about the bond between a mother and her child very differently. I related that bond to the moment a mother sees her child for the first time, skin to skin, breastfeeding.

After making the decision to adopt children, I asked myself how I would be able to create a connection with my child if we didn't have these experiences? Every time I asked myself this, I could feel my heart beating a little stronger.

Even before meeting my daughter, my heart knew her. We were connected. When I heard my daughter's cry echo through the halls as she was being brought to meet me, my heart broke for her. She must have been so confused, scared and tired. She must have been wondering where she was. There were so many unknowns, but when she came through the door, I immediately knew what to do. I held her and comforted her and wiped her tears. She clung to me even though I was a stranger. I didn't look anything like her. I had different eyes, different skin, and a different smell. She was two years old. She could have fought to leave my arms, but she stayed. I looked at her with kind eyes and a soft touch. I was creating a bond in those first few minutes, and, for me, that was my moment after giving birth.

I was creating a heart to heart connection. She clung to me and slept on my chest and I believe she felt safe and comforted. This was the beginning of a beautiful relationship.

Growing up in Maine during the 70s and 80s, I was very isolated from the outside world. I went to Catholic School until 8th grade and often didn't feel like I had a lot of adults to talk to. I used to feel that my voice didn't matter and that my questions didn't need answering. I was lonely. I did not grow up around a lot of diversity and there seemed to be only one way of thinking. I wanted to question things but was quickly reminded that I was to be seen and not heard. No one took the time to explain why things worked a certain way. I wasn't living a life of clarity, so my heart was closed off throughout my childhood. These are the years that would become most important as I became a mother. I had an understanding of how it felt to not be heard. I knew what it felt like to cry myself to sleep and not know where your place in this home, school or world was. These years would help me to become the mother that I am today. Showing patience, allowing my children to lead in what they need in a moment.

At the age of 23, I was ready to step out of small-town living and small-time thinking. I was nervous but so ready to step into the unknown and to have this opportunity. By doing so, I would be exposed to a whole new world of adventures through my life as a flight attendant. Meeting new people and learning about other religions, sexualities and races really exposed me to just how sheltered I had been growing up. I can recall being afraid around what I didn't understand or how others lived. Reflecting on that time, I am so grateful for that time in my life. I took a chance on myself and sought the answers so that I could come with an open heart and open mind. It felt so good to be getting answers. I was finding my way in young adulthood.

Having clarity was important to me especially since adoption was on my heart. I wanted to ensure that I knew who I was before becoming a parent. Our greatest lessons are often the ones we could have benefited from during various stages of our lives. Love and acceptance were not always something that I was shown. I was right where my heart needed to be. I was uncomfortable and I was grateful for the growth in these uncomfortable situations. These moments would help me to become the mother that I wanted to become. I was already setting an example for myself and for my children whom I hadn't even met yet.

I was introduced to my husband during my time as a flight attendant. I recall sharing with him on our first date, my desire to adopt children from China when I turned 30. I also shared with him my intentions of staying home to raise them and wanted to know his feelings about that. Ours wasn't a typical first date conversation. He said he was open to adoption and to having a wife who stayed home to raise the child(ren). This was the first time I was putting exactly what I wanted out into the world and, even though I was a little uncomfortable, it felt so good. In many ways, I can look back and say that this was one of the first times in my life that I had stood up for myself, loved myself and owned my desire to adopt children. I was so excited to meet a man who would share in this journey with me and who had a heart that was open.

I have chosen my family throughout my life. And that required much from my heart, expansion being a prime ingredient. I chose and grew a family that loves fiercely and accepts each other and allows this to be the foundation of our family.

Love and acceptance! How beautiful. I continue to build on this foundation daily and I love how aligned we are together as one.

The moment I became pregnant in my heart with the love of my daughter is a moment I love to share. I was meant to see her picture on the eve of Thanksgiving 2006. And the moment I saw her photo I had an instant connection. I would stare at this photo for the next few days. I had so much hope. So much love for a child that I had never met. I knew nothing about this little girl. I didn't know her story. I didn't need to know. I felt so sure that I was her mother and she was my daughter. I was so excited to call the adoption agency the Monday after Thanksgiving to let them know. I was on cloud nine all weekend and when Monday morning arrived, I was crushed. The adoption agency informed me that adopting this child was not an option since she was with another adoption agency. I requested that we send a letter requesting us to adopt this child.

The weeks that followed are what I call my morning sickness period. I was experiencing less sleep and the thought of not meeting this beautiful human being was making me nauseous. My morning sickness would last for weeks. Then it all changed for me the day a letter came back from China giving us the opportunity to adopt this little girl. I was restored at that moment and the next trimester began. My husband and I were full of hope, love, and excitement. The light was shining from within. Now we just had to wait to get travel approval and we would be off to meet her. Those next few months would seem like an eternity. We decorated a room and started to create a home to welcome her.

We traveled to China in November of 2007. Those two weeks in China brought tears and exhaustion but, most importantly, so much love. We were facing all this newness together as a family of three. We were challenged and maybe questioned

5

what we were doing as new parents. It became easier and easier the more we allowed our hearts to lead the way. We arrived home in the United States on Thanksgiving Day. It was a 12-month journey from seeing a picture to being in our home all together.

To love someone and be accepting of all their gifts is not as easy. I have found that it starts with me. If I am not accepting of all my gifts, it is harder to be accepting towards someone else. When I adopted my children, I knew some of their gifts ahead of time. I started to look within when it came to how I reflect on my differences and gifts so that I would be an example to them. I wanted to provide a home that was a safe place to have the hard discussions. I wanted it to be a place where love was at the center of it all. I also wanted them to know that in this love I would hold their hands and walk through their journey with them side-by-side. We are in constant learning of who we are and what feels good to our hearts.

I have reminded myself, and my children, that who you are is worth celebrating. To look in the mirror and love the person you see. You matter! You are worthy! You are loved just as you are! Love and accept yourself and you will love and accept others in their greatness. Love shines through all of the darkness.

Today, I am raising two middle school children with my husband. Love is at the center of our home. I show up for my children in ways that they need me to. I love the connection that we have, and I am filled with joy as they are finding out who they are. I support them and love them through it all. I stand with them and hold their hand in their journey of life.

Motherhood is a constant evolution and my job as a mom is to:

1. Teach my children how to feel confident in their journey.
2. Help my children celebrate their uniqueness.
3. Raise my kids to love and accept themselves.
4. Guide them through the hardships of other people's perceptions and opinions.
5. Support them as they use their voice.
6. Remind them how important they are in life.
7. Celebrate with them as they share their story.
8. Coach them on their way to learning how to let love be present.
9. Prepare them to let others into their heart.
10. Reinforce their worth.

May these words connect you with your inner child, your own child, and the children of this world. May we all love one another through acceptance.

I remind my children that their opportunity is to be their own best friend. My kids know that in order to love and accept someone else, they must first love and accept themselves.

A self-acceptance exercise I practice with my children often is this:

Place your hand on your heart and close your eyes. Take some deep breaths. Visualize who you are and who you want to be. Love yourself and give yourself a hug. Be gentle on your journey.

We can start this practice at any age and expand our hearts and break down old stories and beliefs that others have put on us.

Love and acceptance lead to more love and human connection. May you give and receive love through true acceptance today.

Birthing from the heart can happen at any age!

And, to my children, you have been two of my greatest teachers in being authentic and loving from the heart. You are a gift and I am grateful to know you both. I love you dearly and my love for you grows. Thank you for choosing me to be your mother!

About Alison Rand

Alison focuses on love and she believes Love Shapes a Family! She has seen how love shows up in different ways through her journey of motherhood. Alison Rand was happy being a stay at home mother and homeschooling her two children. She never expected to be helping other mothers with nutrition until she herself found herself needing guidance. Alison was diagnosed with an autoimmune disease and was seeking answers that would bring her back to her old self. She never expected to find her answers from nutrition and gain more energy, more clarity, weight loss, clearer skin while getting her autoimmune disease under control. As a family, they cook delicious meals with organic wholesome ingredients daily. They have seen firsthand how reading labels and investing in food make a huge difference in how they feel. It has been a blessing how nutrition gives her new hope, new ways and new beginnings. It was only natural to start sharing and blessing others with what she is learning. Alison Rand is a wife and mother to two adopted children. She and her husband moved from Maine to Arizona in 2003. She focuses on love being at the center of her family. As she homeschools her children, she loves seeing them learn and finding their way in this world. Finding their passion and see them share their gifts with others. Alison was a flight attendant when she met her husband in 2000. She loved traveling and exploring so many places she dreamed about in childhood. It was only natural to share traveling with her children. As a family they spend time exploring new states each summer whether by car or by plane. Creating memories as a family!

Alison M. Rand
Love Shapes a Family
602-300-6650
www.alisonmrand.com
alison@alisonmrand.com
Facebook: @ali.rand
Instagram: @Alisonmrand

A Love Letter to My Daughter

by Brita Moe

Dear Alida,

    Until I had you, I did not know what love was. Sometimes I thought I knew, most of the time I struggled to find and understand it. Sometimes I felt I had a broken heart; that must have been an illusion, because, before you, I did not truly love. Until you came along, I thought I had loved, but not fully. Giving birth to you expanded my heart and my soul. When you came along, I saw only love! For the first time, I knew I would die for someone, no questions asked, no hesitation.

Don't get me wrong, my darling. My life prior to you was grand. It was fast-paced and fun. I was living it up with my job as a pilot and I had friends in pockets of the earth where others never get to visit. Yet, I always knew when the time was right that I was to be introduced to a higher dimension of life.

I had heard about this "motherly love" phenomenon before you were born, but I did not know that for me it would trigger such a paradigm shift! In the beginning, this newfound love paralyzed and scared me. The fearless girl who could accomplish anything was diminished. Not because she was in your shadow, that was ok, but because she was now more vulnerable. Before, she was not scared of dying, and now she was, you needed me. I guess the reason that girl was diminished, was because she was supposed to metamorphose into a woman.

You helped me climb up the spiderweb-covered staircase to harness this love, to come out on top stronger and more radiant. You showed me how to be a vulnerable mother, and yet a strong woman. As my heart expanded, it allowed me to love others stronger too, to enjoy life fully, to feel peace, and heal with love! I love your dad on such an unbelievably deep level because of you, which makes us a strong family. Your dad and I look at you and your brother and we see that you are our biggest achievement yet, and we want to give you all the tools you need to live a happy life. You have already shown us that being together as a family is your number one source of joy. Your dad and I know that we are not perfect, and at times will not be perfect parents, but you remind us of how important it is to nurture the love and relationship we have so that we can give you the safest ship to sail in your lives' voyage. This has forced us to grow up, rise above pity and to focus on loving each other. We have seen with our own eyes how making that love-centered decision to always do what's best for the whole family, is like seeing love spread like the herb chocolate mint in your garden. It looks messy, and maybe your house doesn't get chosen for the garden walk, but it's oh so delicious.

You spent a few days at the hospital last week and your dad accompanied you. Your brother and I came to visit you during the day and you were being so brave. You kept up your mood despite being hooked to a breathing machine and being stuck inside a room all day. When your doctor came to take some tests, you introduced her to your 9-month-old brother. You were so proud to show off your whole family unit. The doctor noticed this and said: "This is the age where family becomes so important to the kids, be sure to stay together as a family." And your dad said, "indeed we have already made that pact." We committed on a wholehearted and deeper level when you came along.

This opening of the love valve also opened an expanded world in the form of new senses. Almost like the somewhat annoying "heightened smell" superpower women get when they're pregnant, I now see the same world through different lenses. This beautiful documentary has more vivid and uplifting colors. You bring reality to the cliché: "the best things in life are free."

I have always felt my own mom's love radiate towards me and my siblings, encapsulating us like a protective veil. I had not understood this intense love before I had you. This love that I could always count on to feel safe and valued.

It does not mean I have become a big softy. My daughter Alida, you are not totally off the hook; there are many kinds of love, including but not limited to tough love and self-love. The most important thing is to make sure that the core of the decision is based on love. If love is the intent, the center of the decision/action/reaction, you can't go wrong, you will always choose the right thing. That does not mean softness; you are just taking away the other parasites; greed, jealousy, anger, loneliness, and the biggest bully in the play-box; fear. When we come from a place of love, we create a win-win situation for everyone involved. When you get a big no to eating the whole box of chewable vitamins in one day or chocolate for breakfast, it's only because I want to give you the best tools for this world, I want you to grow up in control of your emotions and with the strength to bounce back.

And grow up you do, so fast, it's a new phase every day. You force me to live in the moment and cherish every minute. If I wanna be present with you in the phase in which you are in, then I need to live in the moment. You remind me that the best part of life is happening right here, right now! Before, too many times, I was either dwelling on the past or dreaming about the future. With you, I can live in the moment and capitalize on the small moments. I know I must grab them and treasure them as-is, move on to the next moment, and always be present in the now. That's how life is indeed supposed to be lived, like a playful child on an adventure in a world filled with magic.

These essential lessons you have taught me, Alida, have made me a better partner, daughter, sister, and friend, for that, thank you! Maybe the homework for humans on this earth-plane is to understand love, and you helped me do just that. Today you are turning two years old, and my maternity leave is soon coming to an end. When you came along someone accidentally hit the fast-forward button times ten, however, thinking back we have accomplished a lot in this timeframe. You have developed so much, you have become a big sister, your 9-month-old brother Sindre looks up to you tremendously and wants to do everything you do.

As much as I love being a pilot, its bittersweet to go back to work. Part of me wants to just be with you and your brother all the time, to hug and protect you. However, I know it's time for me to blend both worlds. To go back to flying airplanes, to feel the fulfillment of doing what I love so I can be the role model you need growing up. And like Winnie the Pooh says; "How **lucky** I **am** to **have** something that makes saying goodbye so hard." I suppose self-love plays its part here. The great unconditional love we feel can truly be all-consuming and, if not careful, you may delete yourself. I hope and pray I can do the balancing act of being me and also be the mother you need at all stages of your life. I will surely do the best I can for you to feel and understand self-love, as that will enable you to be strong and empathic. I am eager to watch how my lessons as a mother enhance my life as a pilot. I understand people in a new way now that I am a mother.

Rest assured, whenever I am up in the sky watching a sunrise, shooting stars, or circular rainbows, I will think of you, your brother and your dad, and I will hurry back as soon as I can. We belong together as a family, and, my dear, I see how important it is for you when all four of us are together laughing and playing. You and your brother are my shooting stars, my deepest source of gratitude.

Many will shut the love valve off to protect themselves, I know I have had it set to half flow at times. It made me harder, tougher, less sensitive, in some ways stronger. It takes bravery to fully love and still feel safe. Too many don't allow themselves to fully love because they're protecting themselves. I can only imagine children growing up in war, what kind of coping mechanism they must have in place. What kind of fear of love must be present? Keep the love valve open, not shut. Because a person who can love fully is also someone who, as a collective, can contribute to healing the world. I already see you doing so beautifully.

What beauty it is to be your mom Alida. I think the medicine the world needs is a light drizzle of motherly love.
Love,
Your mother

About Brita Moe

Brita Moe is a dynamic entrepreneur, multilingual pilot, and inventor. Having come to the United States as a young adult pursuing a degree in aviation, she founded an aviation company. She went on to become a captain in the airline industry. During those pursuits, she continued her entrepreneurial path receiving certifications in business and entrepreneurship. Expanding her portfolio into real estate, she runs a successful rental company focusing on high-end properties to provide an oasis from the everyday stressors of work life. In addition, she has two beautiful small children and a supportive partner. They split their time between the lowland fjords of Norway and the Rust Belt in America.

Twinkle Twinkle, You Are Loved

by Pauline Erickson

WHEN WE BECOME MOMS, WE OPEN OURSELVES UP TO experiencing a whole new range of emotions. We become superhumans who can transcend from one emotion to the next while leaping over obstacles and balancing a to-do list, all while keeping our priorities top of mind. As moms, we briefly put our feelings aside and, out of profound love, we put our children's needs first. We do well to remember that love is always the answer.

Becoming a mom was a bit of a roller coaster ride for me. Pregnant—not pregnant, pregnant—not pregnant, pregnant—not pregnant, pregnant—not pregnant, pregnant—BABY GIRL!

What a privilege and honor it was to finally become a mom. January 13, 2011 was the day our eyes met as she laid on my bare chest for the first time with her eyes staring up at mine. It was an intense connection that happened in a split second and reached down deep within my heart. Her father and I embraced this journey with hearts full of gratitude. Our hopes and prayers had been answered.

Our life as a family of three is ever-expanding with new visions of our future ahead of us. We thought a sibling for Isabelle, making us a family of four, would be our next natural experience of joy. Back on a roller-coaster ride, we go. At some point in the ride, I was waiting in our parked car outside a store with my daughter, who was four at the time, when a minivan parked alongside us suddenly came alive with the sound of kids' laughter and joyful shouts. There were laughing children jumping and playing about as they loaded themselves into the van. The mom was busy with an infant and car seat as the other four happy children loudly played amongst themselves. Meanwhile, as they were settling in, I noticed in my backseat, my one and only child staring at them as though she were in another world.

At this point in my roller coaster ride, I too, felt like I was in another world watching the nearby mother with her infant child. Had things gone a little differently, that could have been me. Not long before, I had lost yet another pregnancy. Quite suddenly, my grief-filled internal dialog was interrupted by a forlorn little voice with a heart-breaking message.

"I wish I was in that family!"

I felt an instant stab in my heart and all my, "I am not good enough" triggers began to go off. I felt my eyes wince, my face flush, my stomach sink, and my lips seal closed while I struggled to take a breath. It felt like a huge frozen moment where time seemed to stop and become defined for both of us. I exhaled and paused long enough to acknowledge my feelings. I asked myself what was true at that moment? What did I really believe? What did I want her to believe? I had a direct communication line from my heart to my head and back to my heart again. I could feel my body begin to relax as I gained control over my emotional body. All this mindfulness and processing was happening in a matter of seconds because my daughter's outcry now demanded my presence and attention. Using my intuition, I needed to tap into my own inner wisdom while putting aside all my would've, could've, should've. As quickly as possible, I decided to show up with gentle strength while putting aside my own self-pity and answer the call of her cry.

She needed me at that moment to show up for her, to remind her of how much she is loved.

We all need that at times. I know I have needed that gentle reminder of truth. The truth that we are loved and never alone.

I asked my higher power for wisdom and guidance in a quick, quiet moment. And in a flash, supermom appeared.

In a gentle understanding voice, I said, "I know. I know you wish you had brothers and sisters that you could play with and you feel sad right now. But mommy and daddy would be so sad if you weren't our daughter and were in another family instead. We love you so much!"

She started to bawl as she realized what she had wished for, not realizing that she was removing herself from her existing life with us, if only in her mind. She did not realize that as she was longing for what someone else had, she was closing off to her own blessings.

She jumped out of her seat and leaped into my lap. We healed each other with a loving embrace. I too needed to be reminded of how much I was loved. I was loved no matter my successes or failures in life. That no matter how different life looked and felt like compared to my expectations, we were loved. And from that, we can give love and receive love more abundantly.

Again, our eyes locked and I shared with her how mommy and daddy have tried to have another child, a brother or sister, but it just hasn't happened yet and it may never happen that way. I don't always know why life is the way it is, but I do know that I can trust that God has a plan for our good, and a future full of hope.

I told my daughter that we are loved and we have our own unique life and purpose. If it is meant for her to be an only child, it will be for some good that we don't yet understand. As I continued to point out to her all the good things about being an only child, she appeared more at peace.

I believe there are times like that one where I get to speak wisdom, hope, and love into her life. We get to connect as a family and grow together in greater understanding and love. But just the same, I am always learning and growing in my heart and spirit from her as well.

We get to remind each other that we are strong, we are loved and we are beyond enough. Each of us has our own unique qualities, strengths and talents to help us live out our life's purpose. There is no one else here on earth exactly like us. How wonderful it is to be with others who get our personalities and recognize, encourage, and support our growth throughout our lives.

Fast forward from age four to eight when I witnessed one of her strengths; patient persistence and determination as she went after her vision with courage and confidence. She had an idea that she would design a playhouse for herself and her puppy, and that her daddy was going to build it. She asked her daddy and he said, "No." She asked again. And again, he said, "No." She asked, "Why not?" Daddy explained that it would soon be dark and so it was not a good time to start a project. But again, Isabelle continued to state her desire and plead her case. Daddy became quiet and his eight-year-old daughter continued to announce her plans and that she really wanted him to help her build it. She continued to ask yet again adding a string of pleases. Daddy was won over.

Mixed with my own emotions, I was speechless. I couldn't decide if I was more upset with him for giving in or impressed with her for the power and confidence in which she went after what she wanted.

The next morning when my emotions had settled and it was just Isabelle and I at home together, I asked her how it was that she had gotten her daddy to say "yes" to building her playhouse? She didn't understand my question and I had to remind her of how she had asked and been told "No" many times. She simply answered that she knew that if she kept asking, he would get tired of her asking and he would eventually say yes.

I smiled to myself as I was reminded by my daughter what quiet confidence and subtle power looked like when led by a persistent childlike desire.

I realized how the many obstacles and setbacks in life over and through all the years had cast an illusion, a sort of shadow on my true self. I had forgotten my own power, at times so easily. If I could only remember to see the world as a child does more often. As a child full of passion, one who is loved and supported in a universe that wants to say yes to me more often if I just keep asking.

As a mom, I protect, care for and teach my daughter daily, but I am at my best when I remember that I am not perfect and she does not expect me to be. I model many things, some of which are humility, love for others and self-respect. Often in this life of mine, feelings, and thoughts of not being enough show up to taunt me. And, it is in these times that I don't have to be super mom. I can be a human who is still learning and growing in love.

I can truly be imperfect me and model what it looks like to accept myself, acknowledge when I am wrong, speak my truth and be confident in my own strengths and path in life. I get to choose to model higher ways of kindness, gratitude, forgiveness, courage, and respect not because I am perfect or even good enough but because of love. It is from a place of love for her and love for myself that I truly see the unique shining stars that we are.

About Pauline Erickson

Pauline Erickson is a Strategic Intervention and Life Happiness Coach helping individuals follow their hearts and create the change they want to make so they can move forward with less anxiety and more pure joy! Pauline understands the challenges of balancing loving others while being true to self. The queen of not giving up, she grew resilience by facing down criticism, shame, self-doubt, frustration, fear and sadness throughout her journey of multiple miscarriages. By holding fast to hope, practicing healing self-care strategies and harnessing her own personal strengths, Pauline stayed strong in the storm to come through it with more peace, passion and purpose. Her mission is to inspire hope and empower the compassionate leader in every woman as she embraces her unique and BeYOUtiful self. In addition to her 24-year career serving thousands as a Licensed Massage Therapist and

Yoga/meditation teacher, Pauline offers; personalized/ group coaching and mind-body training programs that support healing, spiritual development and personal growth. She helps her clients discover their strengths, believe in their dreams and grow in love for themselves and others as they share their talents and gifts with the world. Living in Woodland, Washington with her loving, strong-hearted husband of 14 years and their sweet daughter, Pauline enjoys good mysteries, coffee chats, and finding hidden treasures while traveling, star gazing, hiking, strolling flower gardens or getting her hands dirty in her own yard. Life is naturally full of wonder and beauty. Join Pauline and break away from chaos! Give yourself a healthy "time-out" to relax your body, renew your mind, and even dream a little here at her website, www.PaulineErickson.com. Be sure to check out her free healing meditation, connect with others in supportive community or sign up for a free clarity session.

All Little Ants Need Their Mother

by Valerie Nifora

I REMEMBER SITTING WITH MY MOTHER AS A LITTLE GIRL on the apartment steps. The sun shone through the window, casting odd shadows on the walls and the floor around us. My mother was busy cleaning the greens she had collected with a sharp knife and a plastic bag, cutting the roots and ends of the dandelions she had gathered. From the bag that lay on the step with discarded roots and earth were little tiny ants scattering about.

"Where are the ants going?" I asked.

"To their homes," my mother answered without looking up. She had her dark hair piled up on her head in a bun and the sun glimmered on the hairpin that kept it all in place.

"What about the baby ants? Where are they going?" I asked concerned.

"To find their mother." My mother answered.

"How will they find their mother?" I asked upset.

"Oh, she leaves a trail for them to follow," my mother answered me looking up this time. "They'll be alright."

"That's good. They need their mother," I responded, satisfied.

We lived in a welfare building on Main Street in a town in New York where my parents had emigrated from Greece. We lived on the second floor tucked away in a corner. It was an old pre-war building with exposed pipes that hissed, floors that creaked, and three locks on the door. But my mother did an incredible job of keeping the home tidy and inviting. She sewed little skirts to hide the unsightly pipes under the sinks. She sewed curtains for old built-in cabinets and windows. And she made sure everything sparkled. My mother took the sadness of the outside world and shut it out, making sure that our inside world was safe. It was here that I learned that you build the world you choose to live in and that anyone can be greater than their circumstances.

For her part, my mother was born during World War II in a village high in the mountains in Greece called Kalithea, north of the isthmus of Corinth. There was always great debate surrounding whether she was born in March or April, as no one seemed to recall the day or time or month she was born. At least, they were certain about the year.

When she was a toddler, she hid in caves while the war waged on and villages were burned to the ground. And when the liberation came, complete with airdrops of food, provisions and vaccinations, she learned to keep the American flag close to her heart and eventually found her way to the United States.

My mother grew up poor—very poor. Regular meals were rare. She had one dress that she wore and that her mother mended with whatever scraps she could find or with scrapes the neighbors had discarded. And she had shoes—mostly—growing up—one pair as it were. She can't say her brother was as fortunate. She was a sickly child which caused additional distress to an already difficult situation. I recall hearing stories of selling the one goat to pay the doctor and other such things. Whatever it was that was done, it seems to have worked because, as of this writing, my mother is alive and well and 78 years of age.

You'd think that her upbringing and perhaps our circumstances in poverty, would have encouraged a spirit of hoarding, or saving, or penny-pinching. But, no – in fact it caused the complete opposite. My mother was always generous and kind to anyone who reminded her of the circumstances from which she came from. Coming to the United States, she hoped to rise above and beyond that poverty. We didn't have much growing up, but my mother's first lesson to me and my sister was one of gratitude and generosity. She often said that anyone at any point in time could easily end up homeless and that all life needed to do was to send you a bad turn. She encouraged us to be grateful for what we had. If we had something to wear, something to eat, and heat in the home, then, my mother assured us, we were better off than many people. And if we had a few coins left in our pockets, she'd remind us to buy food for anyone we saw who needed it. She taught us to look people in the eye when we spoke to them because no one was ever beneath us nor above us. We were all just human.

My mother's lessons of humility often found us at the local thrift store. If there was any extra money, my sister and I were allowed to look for a discarded toy we could buy for a quarter. There was no shame. We were grateful that we had the ability to buy from there. There were other children who didn't even have this privilege. And, I must tell you that my favorite toy, to this day, was a multi-colored xylophone my sister had selected. It didn't have a mallet, which made it all the more fun as we improvised with spoons, pencils and all other sorts of items we could find—the sounds were different depending on what we used, and we delighted in this greatly.

When I was in third grade, my parents saved enough money that allowed us to move to a nicer and safer neighborhood. We wound up in a small Cape Cod on the corner of the block where a large pine tree stood; we always thought it needed a star at Christmas. I have a very distinctive memory of driving away from our old brick building thinking that my parents had managed salvation. In our old neighborhood, there were police raids and all sorts of crimes that I can categorize now as an adult, but I didn't fully understand their gravity as a child. All I knew was that these things frightened me. It was in buying the house where my parents still live to this day that my mother taught me the fine art of resilience.

It took her and my father almost a decade to save enough money to buy the small house. The building on our old neighborhood had changed a lot over the years, and although many of their friends had left and found refuge elsewhere, we were the last ones to go. My mother had a large hand in ensuring that we left. She did so by teaching herself how to sew. I'm not exactly sure how she saved enough money to purchase the Singer sewing machine that she still owns and uses to this day, but I can tell you that that Singer sewing machine and my mother's self-taught sewing skills were our salvation from poverty.

She made our clothes with that machine. I remember lovely dresses that were hand embroidered. One time in Kindergarten, my teacher had me sit on a chair during reading time so as not to ruin my dress. That made me feel special.

Over the years, there were many illnesses, job losses and other unfortunate things that happened, but my parents always managed to get through it. We always ate. There was always heat. And we were always safe. Resiliency is a life-long process where you struggle to keep swimming even if the waves keep coming.

My mother is a fighter, even to this day. I would not recommend arguing with her because my money is betting on her winning. One thing my mother could never tolerate was to be insulted or to have someone else insulted for their shortcomings or as a form of personal attack. My favorite story about this involves an incident with a telephone worker who didn't have the patience to listen to my mother's thick accent over the phone. The customer service rep made the mistake of telling my mother to "learn better English" and then hung up on her. This is back in the '70s when you could easily drive to the telephone building and actually speak to a customer service rep—which my mother did—little me and my little sister in tow. Anger always gave my mother laser-sharp focus, and I cringed slightly when she not only found that person, but lectured them on how she knew Greek very well, and English was something she was learning and how about this particular person try learning Greek? It did elicit an apology. My mother has this magical way of having people make peace with her, even if they annoyed her, and so the issue ended up being resolved amicably. All my mother wanted was fairness, that's what she was seeking, and I think most people sensed and respected that.

Even last week, when she found herself in the hospital (yes, she'll be ok), she was good enough to tell the nurse who was managing her, that she needed to slow down and explain what she was saying to my mother so that she could understand it. And my mother didn't care how long it took, but she was to have patience and let my mother ask questions. Again, I thought cringe-worthy, but this nurse told me how Mom was right, and that she'll miss her. So, there's that.

My mother's general perspective when things are unfair is that "You have to fight about it. Move!" To which, my sister took greatly to heart when she became a very successful attorney.

Like most things in her life, my mother was before her time. She taught me about wage disparities even before it became a thing women vocally fought for. When it came to her attention that she wasn't being paid the same as the male tailors even though her work was far more superior (It honestly was, and people, would specifically ask for my mother to alter their suits), she marched herself into her boss's office and informed him that he had about a week to consider what her raise was going to be before she quit. Did we need the money? Yes! Was she going to quit? Yes! Did she have a plan B? Of course. She also informed him with her lovely accent, that, "I'm talking dollars not cents." After the shock wore off, her boss delivered on time per her deadline. She did get her raise and it was on par with what she had asked for. And she didn't quit.

She tried desperately to teach herself to read. Between working nights and not qualifying for "public programs," my mother would sit with me as a young child and watch me struggle to read. But, not one to allow circumstances to limit her, she decided she would teach herself to read while I was also learning how to read. "How do you say that word?" she would ask. "What does that word mean that I heard on the TV?" "What sound does that letter make? Why is it this way and not another sound?" As I learned to read English, she learned to read in English. She is essentially an elementary school level reader, but it was all through her own efforts. About which, I am immensely proud of her to this day.

I could easily go on and on and on about my mother. There is no one like her. And, there will never be anyone like her. I often struggle with what the world will be like when she departs it. To say that there will be an enormous chasm is not an understatement. Anyone who has spent time with my mother will tell you that she is wise, kind, complicated, and right. She taught me and my sister that self-confidence, self-worth, and self-discipline were by far the most important characteristics in life. Generosity, forgiveness, reliance, were the keys to a meaningful life.

My mother showed us a world of possibilities in life, not limits. A life where every little ant always found its way home. Because mothers are important.

About Valerie Nifora

Valerie Nifora was born and raised in New York to Greek immigrant parents. For over twenty years, she served as an award-winning Marketing Communications Leader for a Fortune 50 company. She has been a ghostwriter for several executives using her special gift as a storyteller to inspire. Her first book, *I Asked the Wind: A Collection of Romantic Poetry,* explores the innocence, sensuality, passion, desire, heartbreak and loss through the lens of her personal experiences spanning 15 years. Her beautiful and powerful voice immediately calls forth a time of leather-bound books and invites the reader to find a comfortable chair and begin their journey through the powerful human emotion of love. The collection was awarded a 5 out of

5-star review from The San Francisco Book Review, "Nifora's poetry flows across the pages, wooing readers from one section to another." Valerie holds a B.A. in Communications from Emerson College and an M.B.A. from Fordham University. She is married and a mother of two amazing sons.

Creando Una Casa
(Creating a Home)

by Nancy Brooker

W E GREW UP IN 'THE WARD,' A LITTLE ITALY IN MY
hometown of Guelph, Ontario. At least 90% of my
neighbors were Italian and most of the moms in the neighborhood stayed home with their young kids.

My mom, Lidia Miotto, was born the youngest of three
children, (Albino, Caterina, and Lidia) to Corina Bordin and
Giovanni Baldin in 1935 in Vedelago, Italy. By the time she
was four years old, both her parents had passed away. Luckily,
her Zia (Aunt) Emilia, fought for mom to be raised by her. My
mom remembers growing up in a very loving home provided
by her Zia Emilia and her husband and always being accepted
as one of Emilia's own children. When she was just 20, she
moved to Canada to marry her sweetheart, my father, who
had come two years earlier.

Mom has affected the way I do everything, from connecting
with others to being a mom, to my health, wellness, fitness

and even fashion. She inspires everyone she meets with her strength, loyalty and grace.

Once my parents were married, one of their top priorities was to build a house. Like so many other immigrants, they did this brick by brick, only as they could afford to, doing a lot of the work on their own and with the help of the Italian community. Mom even tiled the floor with my uncle. Using the valance from a trapunta (quilt) on their bed, she made curtains for the windows. She made pillows and beautiful clothes for all of us. And of course, she made 'Italian skates', knitted slippers that we used to slide all over the house.

Growing up, I'd always help my mom hang the laundry outside during summer. The breeze and the sun and the smell of clean clothes floating in the air brought me a feeling of ease and joy, like having a warm, fresh blanket wrapped around me. My mom made everything feel warm and safe. Those days were so perfect that I wouldn't fuss too much when she made me help her iron the sheets and underwear while watching her favorite soap, Another World.

I still hang my laundry to air dry outside any chance I get and will often stop and just breathe in the smell of laundry fresh off the line, traveling back in time to my childhood days. I've decided to pass on ironing the underwear though.

Mom stayed home until I started kindergarten. Even working, she found a way to make us feel loved and safe. Growing up with an Italian mom does involve lots of homemade, really amazing food. School lunch breaks, while we didn't eat gourmet food, were still a point for my mom to stop her busy day and focus on us kids. My siblings and I would walk home from school, picking mom up at her work along the way. We'd all go home and enjoy a bowl of soup before returning to our busy days.

Even though my mom went back to work once I started school, I remember making a decision at a young age that when I had children, I would stay at home with them too. I didn't manage to be a full-time stay-at-home mom, but I came pretty close to being one.

Italian Food Makes a Home

With Italians, where there are family and friends, there must be good food. It's ingrained in our upbringing. My mom is an amazing cook, just ask my kids! As a child, I remember all the Italian neighbors doing things at the same time. They all made their own wine at the same time, homemade salami, and plucking the farm bought chickens. The smells in our house ranged from heavenly—delicious chicken soup and minestrone, homemade pasta sauce and rabbit, to burnt chicken feathers and fishy baccala.

My mom didn't learn to cook until she moved to Canada and her Italian friends and relatives passed down family recipes. This amazed me as everyone assumes that I learned to cook incredible food growing up in an Italian home, but neither my sister nor I learned to cook until after we left home. Mom has always been there for us with her crazy half-written recipes though.

When my oldest son Jacob was in fourth grade, he had to do a photo essay on how to make something. He chose to photograph 'How to Make Fugasa' (a yummy Italian Easter Bread). We got the basic ingredients by phone from my mom and on a blustery Canadian winter day over the March break, I gathered my niece and nephew and my three kids and we all ventured out to the grocery store to buy them. Jake took photos (wide lens, closeups, etc.) of everyone picking ingredients off the shelves, and the next day, my mom came over with her recipe so they could make it together. Of course, the recipe itself was in Italian and barely legible from all the food stains from the many, many years of use!

My mom brought the secret ingredient (Spummadoro from Castelfranco, a town just outside her hometown of Vedelago), and went through her routine, grabbing dirty cups from the sink to measure with because Italians reuse everything. She moved like a whirlwind while Jake tried to keep up with step by step photos of the process. Fugasa is an Italian Easter Bread, so it must be kneaded with great strength and great care, and then left to rise in a warm and quiet place for several hours before cooking. That last part was an even more difficult task with five kids at my house, but we managed to bake three delicious cakes. The kids had a ball and it was just another thing that my mom could do that amazed and awed us all.

I found it frustrating that I couldn't follow an exact recipe, but it was so in line with how she lives. She taught me to make the best use of what I have and be flexible enough to move through challenges to my endpoint. Jake got a 4+ (a perfect mark) on his photo essay, we ended up with an actual English legible version of this delicious traditional recipe, and we had so much fun in the kitchen with my mom.

I'd go on to do this repeatedly with several traditional Italian foods, like her amazing lemon cookies and bistecca impanati (breaded veal cutlets). I broke my rolling pin the first time I tried to follow the cookie recipe I created from mom's lemon cookie demonstration.

Mom could easily have been a nutritionist or some kind of health care worker. In Italy, she learned how to pick edible mushrooms. Nowadays, my kids are still not sure how that skill translated to Canadian mushrooms. As a kid, I remember her picking mushrooms and edible weeds. We had a breadman, an egg lady, a milkman, the Vita Gingerella guy (pop) and even an Italian underwear guy who would come to the neighborhood. While the Italian adults were buying undergarments, the kids of the block looked forward to the chiclets gum he handed out.

We even had an elderly Italian neighbor who picked snails after any downpour of rain and delivered them to the neighborhood. I helped my mom cook by using a needle to pick the snails out of their shell so she could work her magic with them! Although I loved the smell of the snails cooked in butter and garlic, I did not love the texture and refused to eat them!

Many days, at lunch, we'd have homemade brodo (chicken soup) and carne lessa (boiled meat) with fresh bread and tomatoes. Back then I was tired of having it so often, but these days I'd kill to have it! Many Fridays I still go over to my parents' home for lunch for homemade minestrone or brodo. Now people pay to have bone broth delivered to their homes in supplements, and I was getting it almost daily as a kid from my ever so wise mom, and not appreciating it.

And of course, we always had a huge vegetable garden in the backyard. To this day, I still go over a few times a week in the summer and take my bag up and down the vegetable aisles in the backyard, picking the freshest and tastiest produce around.

As a kid, most Sundays in the summer, we'd convoy to the beach, go to mass at the Church near our usual spot, and then enjoy a day of sun and feasting. We'd eat things like Bistecca Impanati and always loads of anguria (watermelon). Even during our cottage vacations, the moms would get together and bake crostoli (a fried Italian pastry)! It must be in my blood though, because for 25 years my husband, kids and I have been cottaging with dear friends, always eating like kings and queens.

We washed and reused milk bags and rainwater, and no piece of food ever went to waste as it could always go into some sort of stew or soup or risotto.

Although I didn't appreciate it as a kid, as a mom and a grown-up now, I learned so much from my mom about whole foods and the value of real, fresh ingredients and good home-made cooking.

Health Matters at Any Age

At 84 and even with a bad knee, my mom is a dynamo. She has been my whole life. It's not that she ever 'worked out' or went to a gym. Her life was a workout, filled with gardening, cleaning, working, walking and riding her bike. Our cottage crew all have fond memories of Nonno and Nonna (Grandpa and Grandma) coming to visit us, and then stealing away on our bikes to get some exercise. My mom, of course, would be wearing a pressed skirt with nylons and nice shoes! Into her 70s she would still throw a football around with the kids. It's not unusual at a family gathering, even to this day, for her and my dad to fight over who gets to walk on the treadmill after supper in the cold winter months. Her energy seems boundless. These days she goes to 'gymnastica' (exercise class) three times a week with my brother. I'm not sure if she needs it with her busy lifestyle, but it keeps them both moving. My mom taught me to treat my body well, to take care of my body so it could take care of me. I'm not sure I'll ever have as much energy as she has, but I'm giving it my best shot, and trying to set the same incredible example for my children.

Passing it Down a Generation

My Italian friends had similar experiences, but one thing that was different in our house was that my brother was diagnosed with type 1 diabetes around age seven. This made it even more important that healthy living was part of everyday life. I have a child who was diagnosed with ADHD and a learning disability around that same age. But as hard as that was for me, this is the age of Google and so there are many options around treatment, plus English is my first language. Even as I ask her about it now, it brings tears to her eyes to remember those days, and all the hardships my brother has had to bear as a result of this disease. I can't imagine what it was like for her to be told her son had a life-threatening illness and not have the language, technology or support network to help her support her child. Back then, dads were not as involved with kids, so she had a lot of responsibility.

Again, I just couldn't even understand the magnitude of the effect this had on both my mom and dad. There were doctors' appointments and insulin to worry about, planning appropriate meals, and dealing with the fallout of insulin reactions. Yet she handled it like she does everything, with incredible strength, dedication and grace under pressure. My brother's doctors still to this day comment that my mom could have been in healthcare given the incredible job she does as his caregiver. For me, this definitely puts into perspective the challenges I face with my own kids with modern healthcare, a supportive husband, and many options for care.

When my youngest was diagnosed with ADHD, I started a Halloween food tradition of my own that continues today. We affectionately call it 'Spooky Dinner.' I wouldn't mistake it for a healthy dinner, but it was my attempt to take the focus off the sweets. It started about 18 years ago with a Mummboli, a homemade panzerotti pizza that looks like a mummy. Over the years, we added Witch's Fingers, Green Monster Toes and Bat Wings (using chlorophyll to make them green and black),

Spider Deviled Eggs, Barfing Pumpkins, even Pumpkin Soup cooked in the pumpkin. My mom was my biggest supporter as I cut out artificial sweeteners, preservatives and moved towards good old-fashioned home-cooked meals. When we tried spelt pasta dough, she started making it from scratch. When we tried goat cheese instead of cow cheese, she always made sure she had some in her fridge for his visits. I know she could see herself in my struggle and wanted to help in any way she could, and that support really got me through some difficult times.

When my parents celebrated their 50th wedding anniversary, my sister and I and our children co-created a video for them in their honor. It was set up as a news report, with segments on everything we love about Nonni (Grandpa and Grandma). The grandkids were the anchors. The traffic report told the story of my mom's fearless journey to Canada, and the closeness of the Italian community through the Italian Canadian Club. The food report showcased the importance of healthy eating, using a segment on gardening (of course featuring pictures of mom and dad working in the garden) and some of our favorite Italian foods. They even included shots of the kids hopelessly trying to bake, covered in flour and wearing pots on their heads, really to show they realize what she does is a skill.

There was Sports, where they showed themselves waterskiing while quoting Nonni on the importance of movement as they were being interviewed. They cut to cameo'd treadmill shots of mom. The fashion report highlighted the respect we all have for mom's skills as a seamstress as the kids made up a fashion house that was courting Nonna.

The weather report talked about the hurricane coming in. My dad (understandably exhausted when we were kids) could have a temper, but with the calming effects of Lidia to offset it.

It was a labor of love and we all absolutely treasure the video and the people who inspired us to make it. Through her actions, my mom has shown us how to be fearless in pursuing a better life, the importance of family and tradition, the importance of healthy eating and exercise, how to be resilient through crises, how to be kind and loving to everyone and how to move with grace the entire time.

I recently had an opportunity to ask her what it was like to leave her family and move to Canada. I always assumed it was traumatic because I would have been filled with fear to move to a new country where I didn't know the language and had very little money to start a new life. My mom laughed when I asked. "I never really thought about it. My brother and Zia were there, and so was your dad. I just didn't know how big Canada was, but I knew it would be ok," she said.

To her, it was an adventure. She took a 17-hour plane ride with only an orange given to her by a kind stranger, to go off to a new land where there would be new friends and new adventures. I've always known my mom to be full of energy and creativity, and strong, but I never thought of her as an adventurer. Even now, she is teaching me to trust my gut and that everything will be ok.

Here in Canada, they carried forward a Canadianized version of the old-world traditions that I feel blessed to have witnessed. I love that my kids have had the luxury of experiencing and learning from them.

Mom, there really are no words for how much you mean to us. We love you.

About Nancy Brooker

For more than 40 years, Nancy lived from a place of fear, scared to use her voice, scared of not living up to what other people expected of her, scared to take risks. A diagnosis of Graves Disease changed everything … even her body was telling her to find her voice, to trust herself, and to take a risk. So Nancy took control of her health … doing the research, talking to the experts but in the end, trusting her gut and doing what was right for her. Even though she had a dismal prognosis from her doctor, she is now 6+ years in remission and feels blessed to have found her voice. Through her private coaching practice, public speaking and workshops, she now helps others reclaim authenticity and purpose in all aspects of their lives so they can move forward with calm, confidence and a renewed energy for living. Nancy lives in Guelph, Ontario with her 4 favorite men—her incredible husband of 28 years and their three amazing sons. Book your complimentary Clarity Call at www.nancybrooker.ca and get your free copy of *7 Simple Ways to De-Stress*.

Nancy Brooker, Certified Master Life Coach
www.nancybrooker.ca
clarity@nancybrooker.ca

Share

by Cori Edwards

M Y MOM CONSCIOUSLY TAUGHT ME MANY THINGS IN LIFE, like how to straighten my socks for church, brush my hair, say please and thank you, and to "not make a mess". Both my parents also told me and my siblings what not to do. I think many parents do not want their children to make the same mistakes that they made. My parents were no exceptions. They let me know what not to do, so I would not make the same mistakes they made. After all was said and done, I realized that the most important lesson my mom taught me was not a deliberate choice. It just happened. And it was beautiful.

I was told the story of Mom through various stories. Marcella Ellada Hulsey had been in many beauty pageants. My mom was born in Rio Hondo, Texas and met my dad in college. They moved to Arlington, Texas, then back to Harlingen, Texas where my dad grew up. Throughout her life, my mom had various illnesses. She had Rheumatic fever twice in her twenties that left her with a heart condition and a full set of dentures. She was never supposed to have children because her doctor said that she would not live through childbirth.

But she proved him wrong. My mom gave birth to my older sister on October 20, 1972. And one year, eleven months and 29 days later, my mom gave birth to me on October 19, 1974. My two-year-old sister thought she got me for her birthday! My mom did come close to dying during my birth, and she had a hysterectomy scar to remind her that she accepted the risk of having children and won. My mom also had hypoglycemia. Hypoglycemia is a low blood sugar disease that caused her to sleep when she ate bread and half her face went numb if she drank half a beer. She also tended to yell—rage actually. My parents had not chosen an easy life. My dad worked a lot and my mom was a screaming perfectionist. So, in my teenage rebellious years, my relationship with my mom wasn't the best. I could not wait to get out of high school and go to college! Both my father and my mother had quit going to college before they graduated. My dad needed six hours to graduate when he chose to quit, and that was a known regret that he talked about throughout my life. My mother was a semester behind him and quit at the same time. She regretted it as well. My sister has always been amazing and I could never do things as great as she did. (That's the truth, not a disgruntled younger sister. She was just better at academics than me.) My sister graduated from Texas A&M - Kingsville and was already working as a teacher. I think she had the gift of teaching from birth. Now, I too had chosen my career. My parents were so proud that both their daughters would graduate from college and not make the same mistakes they had. Everything was going to be ok.

During my junior year in college, I made some poor choices and drastically damaged my relationship with my mom. I had lost my way during college and that destroyed my mother. She didn't know how to help me, and I didn't want her help. We didn't know how to talk to each other. I was nasty and mean and I didn't like myself.

Luckily, I pulled myself together. I changed my ways. I changed my outlook on life. I changed my friends, my boyfriend, everything. My parents were my own personal cheerleaders. Off I went determined to give 100% to living a thriving, fulfilling life!

During my senior year, I was accepted for a paid internship at The Autism Treatment Center in San Antonio in August 1998. I was working in the education component and loved it. Many of the clients had autism coupled with other brain diseases. This fascinated me and I was so excited to learn more about behavioral therapy and modification. I planned to work there full time after I graduated. Everything was falling into place and life was good!

I can't remember exactly what I was doing when my dad called to tell me that he was in the emergency room with my mom. He said that her body was so swollen that her skin was stretching and hurting. She was being admitted into the hospital and I need not worry—he was just letting me know. He just wanted me to know that she was sick and was being cared for and he would tell me any news as soon as he knew.

I told my manager and team at the Autism Treatment Center what was going on and that I would soon be leaving to drive to my hometown of Harlingen, Texas. They had become my work family and shooed me out the door to go home. I was in good spirits, going home to my mom to help her get well and help my dad take care of her. My mom was tough, and she had so much experience overcoming health issues, that I was not worried.

The days were a blur after I got to the hospital in Harlingen, Texas. It was a crisis. Something was very, very wrong.

I would talk to my dad and could hear the panic in his voice as he tried to comfort my sister and me. I would talk to my sister and we didn't know what to say or feel. The doctors could not figure out what was wrong with her. Something was causing kidney failure—but they didn't know what it was. Something was attacking her kidneys like they were foreign to her body. It was not cancer, and her kidneys were dying. She started her first dialysis. Then she did it again and again while the doctors researched and took blood tests daily. No one knew what was going on. The hospital did a biopsy of her kidneys and we waited anxiously for a report. I drove back to school when I needed to, drove to work when I needed to, and went back every minute I could. We took shifts staying at the hospital with her.

Finally, a doctor came in and told us that he had figured out what was going on.

This is a day that I will never forget.

My mom was diagnosed with scleroderma. Scleroderma is evil. It is cruel. It is soul-sucking and life-taking. The name literally means "hard skin". There is no cure. And the amount of people who have scleroderma in the United States is equivalent to the population of Anchorage, Alaska.

My dad, sister and I would not accept that there wasn't a cure and kept asking the doctor for any updates on treatments. We researched scleroderma and read about cases—they usually all ended in a painful death.

I was so angry. I was angry at my father because he had not taken her to the hospital sooner because we didn't have health insurance. I was angry at the doctor for not knowing how to cure this. I was angry that it took so long for the doctor to figure this out. I was angry that it was a terminal disease and there was no cure. I was angry at the other people who came to the hospital and left while we were there. I was angry at myself because I had been such an asshole to my mom for most of my teen and adult life. I was angry at God—if he even existed.

Scleroderma was the reason that it hurt so much when the nurse drew blood samples from her daily. Scleroderma was the reason that her kidneys were dying and she had to get a permanent dialysis catheter placed in her jugular vein. Scleroderma was the reason my mom told me she was never leaving the hospital alive. Scleroderma was the reason my dad's heart broke and never recovered.

Scleroderma was the reason that all the walls came down and my mom taught me the best lesson in life: Share.

She shared so much of her life with me. She shared how she felt at different ages and the choices she made and why. She told me funny stories and sad stories. She told me that she raised her little brother and how he meant the world to her. I still remember her scream after the phone rang late at night when I was little. I didn't know what was going on. Her little brother had been shot by a man he was chasing into a house in Beaumont. He was an undercover police officer and had chased a known child molester into a building to catch him. The guy shot him in the side through his bulletproof jacket. This broke my mother's heart. I didn't know the depth of that pain until my mother cried and told me how she had lost a part of her. I cried with her in the hospital, finally understanding how she felt that night. She lost her baby brother and that devastated her.

She shared how my grandmother made her the prettiest dresses. She shared how her mother would dress up every day and walk to the Five And Dime in her high heels to report for work. Her mother always had her hair done and took care of herself. She also helped my mother win many beauty pageants.

She was beautiful and had many guys who wanted to date her. She was a class act and was well-known in the community.

I repeatedly asked my mom about her boyfriends before my dad. She told me that she had a serious boyfriend named Mike before she met my father. I recalled a gold charm bracelet that I played with often growing up—but I never knew the story behind it. It was really cool and had a charm shaped like a graduation cap that didn't have a date on it. Another round charm said "A Date To Remember 10–29–65" in cursive and on the back, "Mike". She told me that she loved Mike, but that he wasn't "The one". She shared how hard it was for her to break up with him, knowing that she was breaking his heart. I had heard the other side of this story from my dad. He said that he saw her in the Christian center at college and watched her break up with this guy who was crying and talking to her. So many emotions.

She shared that she had met my dad on a double date and that he was actually her friend's date. She really liked him, and her friend was not into him. She soon found out that he liked her too. She shared the words that triggered the know—without a shadow of a doubt—that she wanted to spend the rest of her life with my dad. It was a moment when he looked at her and told her that he loved her with all his heart. He loved her beyond measure. And also that he would always put God first, and her second. That is the moment when she knew in her heart that she wanted to marry my father. Because God was sacred in her heart as well.

She shared how she felt in college and why she decided to quit. How it didn't feel like a mistake at the time. They made decisions together, as a team. They were best friends. Living this life together. Sometimes things happen and we ban together to resolve them. There is no manual, only love.

48

She shared about getting rheumatic fever twice. It softened all her teeth and she had to get dentures in her early twenties. All of her teeth were unusable. When the doctor told her she should never have kids, that pissed her off. She was having kids and no one was taking that away from her. If she died in childbirth, so be it. But no one was going to tell her that she could not have her own children.

We were the same—mother and daughter. Raw emotions and experiencing life! I was given the gift of really knowing my mom and I was losing her at the same time. I finally understood my mom. All of the stories finally made sense. I will cherish those nights of sharing in the hospital forever. When I miss her, I go back there and remember. She was in a regular hospital room for the first three months, then sedated in ICU for the last three months.

In ICU, they monitored the oxygen in her lungs. Her kidneys were gone and scleroderma had moved to her lungs, attacking them as if they were foreign. She had a breathing tube down her throat and she was on a ventilator. She was in a medically induced coma; I could tell she was in hell and we couldn't fix it. I wished she would just go home. We were going to be ok.

On Friday, December 13th, 1998, I whispered in my mother's ear that I had graduated. I told her that I was driving back to San Marcos to get my diploma, walk across the stage and get my diploma, and then I would drive back home. I would be right back.

I was exhausted when I pulled into my driveway that day, yet I had the most peaceful feeling. My roommate was there waiting for me. I already knew. My mom had finally passed away. She was finally free of that body.

At the end of her life, my mom taught me the greatest life lesson that I will never forget, and today, I do the same with my children: I share. Because I want my kids to know I am human too, that I have felt the way they do. That I didn't understand what was going on when I was little and I also went through puberty. Share your life with those you love.

About Cori Edwards

Cori Dean Edwards is an accomplished independent woman who enjoys empowering people to be the best version of themselves they can be. She didn't understand the true meaning of life until she lost both parents tragically and engaged in a difficult divorce. She learned that happiness is achieved by helping others to know their worth. This has formed the person she is today, the successful single mom who is now buying her own home in a lovely neighborhood with plenty of room for family, friends and loved ones to gather and enjoy life with.

Learning How to Enjoy Life

by Michael Berg

O F ALL THE CHARACTERISTICS ATTRIBUTABLE TO A mother, there is usually one that stands out, something she passes on as a lesson learned. In the case of my mother, it was not something she told me over and over, but something she just did—my mother loved life no matter what she was doing, she still does. I may have been in my 20s before I even realized what a lasting impression this left on me.

My mother, Inger, has always enjoyed most things that come her way, and she is never afraid to learn something new. This is not to say that she loves doing laundry or dishes, but in general, she faces most things with a smile. If she has to learn something new, she just digs in and does it.

She was born in Stockholm in the early '40s and therefore spent her most impressionable years in post-war Sweden when the world was still trying to recover from WWII. Her parents were hardworking people who survived modestly but well. She spent most of her childhood and young adulthood in the same small house just south of Stockholm. This is where she spent her weekdays going to school as well as the long and dark winter months. Her summers and weekends were something entirely different. Her parents had come by a small lot on an island in the archipelago 50 miles east of the city, right where Sweden turns into the Baltic sea. Her father built a small cottage where, even though the weather was less than perfect most of the year, the family spent weekends and summers. She met my dad in her early 20's, and they were inseparable until he passed away a few years ago.

Their journey to the United States started in that small house south of Stockholm and took them to a mountaintop in North Carolina. Along the way, my mother found herself needing new skills, like learning German and later improving her school-level English. There were many things she had to do and learn to get "to there from here," things far outside her comfort zone, but she just trudged on, mostly with a smile on her face.

Memories of my mom from back then are a bit mixed as she played so many different roles in our family. My dad, a serial entrepreneur, traveled a lot and she had to pick up where he left off almost every week. There were lawns to be mowed, things to be painted and eventually also a business to run. It must be mentioned here that I have two younger brothers, so she had to learn to keep up with 3 boys and she rarely got to do any girl stuff.

Shortly after I was born, my parents packed up and moved to Germany for a few years. We spent one year in Munich, and then four years in a suburb of Bonn. My dad's job brought them there and they traveled a good portion of Europe by car with me and my brother Joe, born 13 months after me, in tow. My mom had to learn a new culture, but I think the hardest thing for her was learning German. German is like Spanish in the sense that the words don't come in the right order, at least not if you start out as a Swedish or English speaker. Five years went by quickly, according to her, and she soon found herself back in Stockholm. The draw of the 25,000 islands that make up the Stockholm archipelago was too strong. They both wanted to spend time there but, more importantly, they wanted us, boys, to have the experience. This is where it starts to get interesting as houses on accessible, with emphasis on accessibility, islands don't come cheap. They found a waterfront plot of land on the same island where her parents had a cabin and the deal was done in a hurry. In order to get to the island, they had to drive for close to an hour to get to the marina where they kept their 13-foot boat. Then they had to load the boat with food and, often, building materials before they cast off and crossed three miles of open Baltic Sea. Keep in mind that the Baltic is rough, cold, and unforgiving. Because there was not a marina on the island, for the first year or so we all had to take a small ferry of sorts to get to the other end of the island and then walk. Yes, walk. The island had no electricity and no roads or cars but was only about a mile across. So, they began building and my mom had to pick up some new skills, yet again. There was an enormous Northern Pine tree where the initial small cabin was to be built; not just a few, it was a forest. Mom never picked up a chainsaw, but she probably got close to doing so. Instead what she did was, as limbs were cut off the felled trees, she would drag them to the beach and burn them in what sometimes became a huge fire. Dad cut the trees and Mom burned the branches all while watching two young boys. I know her parents helped a lot, but she was still a very busy woman that summer.

The result was a 15 by 30-foot cabin with no electricity and no running water, but what it lacked in conveniences was made up for by the view. The front of the house faced west and the sunsets were incredible and lasted forever. My mom loved this place. That far north, the sun rises and sets in almost the same place in the summer and the sunset can last for almost a full hour.

For the place to operate, my mother had to learn how to operate the kerosene heaters. She had to carry water in large buckets from a well nearby and she had to relearn how to love using a real outhouse. If anybody needed a bath, they would need to grab the specially formulated "saltwater soap" and get in the water which rarely got to 70F in the summer—never mind the spring and fall.

In order to get the boat to the property, they had to build a dock. This was interesting and extremely hard work. I became familiar with just how hard this work was when repairing and expanding the dock later became a job for me and my brother. My dad would fashion pilings from pines and literally drive them into the mud with a sledgehammer. Once pilings were in place, my Mom would get to work on filling the dock with rocks. It had to be almost full of rocks or the ice, which could get over a foot thick in the winter, would simply carry the dock away. I don't know how many rocks she carried to that dock over the years but there were many, and again, she just loved doing it. I think she believed it was work that needed to be done and you might as well have fun doing it. The cabin was eventually expanded into a four-bedroom house and by that time, both phone service and electricity had arrived in parts of the archipelago.

As all this was happening on weekends and during the summer, there was also a life "in town" as we called it. My brother and I had to go to school and play soccer, ice hockey, golf, ski, and other activities. We were also both Sea Scouts, so there was no lack of activity at any given period. The house we lived in was what could be described as a one-story row-house. The location was great as we could walk to all our schools and there was a forest that began in our back yard and went on for miles. Three houses down was the entrance to a ski and sled-hill that was large enough for us to learn how to ski on. But my parents were not happy with the one-story situation as the family was about to expand and they needed space for a business as well. So here we went again, construction and another boy! Though they had professional help this time, there were still hundreds of things for my mom to do to make it habitable.

When computerized word processors became available, my mom decided on her next move. Together with my dad, she started a company that could do this neat little trick called "mail merge". With large computer discs and daisy wheel printers, they set out to do mailings for different customers. Their ability to print a letter with somebody's name at the top was a brand-new service and everybody wanted to do it. Though there were many late nights and unpleasant deadlines, she was always excited about the work. She did the data entry, the printing, and the stuffing of the envelopes.

In the mid-'80s, my dad was offered a job in Naperville, IL. It was to be a two-year contract which at some point got extended indefinitely making us all permanent residents and immigrants, though we didn't know this at the time. We talked about it as a family extensively and we all thought it sounded like a nice two-year adventure. I remember wondering what the Chicago suburb would be like, but at no point did I stop to think about how this would change the life of this mother of three. She had learned German but her English was what she had learned in school and there was plenty of room for improvement just to be functional. Now, you would think that a family from Sweden would adapt easily to the weather in Chicago—no way. We arrived in January and it was cold, colder than any of us had ever experienced.

My dad was working and traveling and my Mom had to deal with us boys adjusting to new schools and a new language in a new country. My youngest brother probably had it the toughest as he arrived at school the first day without speaking a word of English, and there was not exactly any help available in Swedish. He did have a friend of the family help him for a few days in the beginning and he learned fast. Through all this, my mom had to deal with the school paperwork, homework in a new language, and all kinds of frustrations and normal things that go on in a family. These "normal" things were greatly amplified by the language difficulties but she always had a great attitude and enjoyed the challenge most of the time.

Two years turned into four and we were all legal permanent residents by the time my dad decided it was time for another business. The business was very successful and they eventually traded the beloved house in the archipelago for a house in the Turks & Caicos. We had all tried to go back and use the place in Sweden during the summers, but it just became too hard to keep up with from such a distance. My parents eventually tired of the Chicago weather and moved to Flat Rock, North Carolina. They had lived in two different houses on a mountain golf course before my dad passed away.

My mother, now just past her mid-70s, still has her own house on that same golf course. We can still catch her scraping and painting decks and railings or doing any other project around the house. Some jobs she saves for when one of us visits but anything she can do herself; she will do herself. I firmly believe she is the happiest after she has accomplished something physical and something that involves a brush or a tool. There is no doubt that her ability to enjoy life no matter what she is doing has rubbed off on me and my brothers as we are always working on something and enjoying it. The many places she has been and the journeys she's chosen have brought many challenges, but if somebody was keeping score, there were more smiles and happy moments—and that's all that counts in the end.

About Michael Berg

Michael Berg was born in Stockholm, Sweden in 1968. He spent his first few years in Germany and then moved back to Stockholm when he was five. Growing up in Sweden, he loved to spend time outdoors playing in the woods or being on the water around the endless islands in the archipelago. He was also given an opportunity to learn, hands-on, everything about engines and boat repair and other things mechanical. Michael was an accomplished Sea Scout and learned to love and respect the sea through their activities. In the mid-'80s, his entire family moved from Sweden to Lisle, Illinois where he spent another 10 years going to high school and grinding his way through a few jobs. In the end, he ended up helping his father start a business in the industry of queuing, which was at the time a very fancy take-a-number system used at DMV's and other places where people wait in line. After a short stint in Asheville, North Carolina, he moved on to McKinney, Texas, where he started his own company after his father sold his. As Michael had no shares in his father's company, he felt this was the right way forward. Michael still loves anything outdoors as well as sailing and ice hockey. The sailing in North Texas is somewhat limited but up until just a year ago he was an avid hockey player. Michael will travel almost anywhere and loves to discover new places, especially places with historical significance.

Motherhood Awakens Divine Power, Intuition and Consciousness

by Whitney Mullings

M Y STORY FEELS PLAIN. IT'S NOT ONE OF TRAGEDY, trauma, or violence. I was just a girl from a traditional Chinese family, with both parents still married and two brothers, who immigrated to Canada at ten years old.

My culture favors boys because they are the ones chosen to traditionally carry the family name, honor, and success of their families. This was ingrained in my upbringing, that my existence had no other value than to support the men in my life with house chores!

"Do as my father, the man of the house says."

I remember a time when I was told to scrub the wok while my brothers played out in the backyard.

There was a time when I was told to "shut up" because "it wasn't my place to speak."

Deep down inside, I knew I was meant for more. So when I left my childhood home to create my own life, I made sure to let out the rebel in me by working hard to create a life of my own.

My first real job outside the shopping mall led to me meeting my husband. He admired my ambition, appreciated my independence, and, most of all, lifted my confidence. Together, we finished post-secondary education while working full-time jobs. It was one of my life's biggest achievements when we bought our first house. We were creating a life of our own.

A few years later, we were ready to expand our family. I remember the moment I realized that I had missed my period. My next thought was that I was going to have a baby boy. "He is here," I thought. I just knew it in my heart. I can't recall a time of such assurance in myself ever before. This was the first awakening experience of my own intuition, the connection we all share in energy form.

The day he arrived, I was introduced to my own stamina and physical endurance and experienced a true example of mind over matter. After 36-plus hours of labor, my son and I met and it was pure love.

Every life decision became so clear and precise thereafter because I knew what was important to me. Day-to-day life was clear but it wasn't easy. Becoming a mother tested every relationship, including the one I had known with myself.

As a new mom, I put my baby's every need before my own needs and anyone else's. Motherhood created tunnel vision so that I only saw what I believed was best for my child. The tunnel was so narrow that it did not leave room for doubt or mistakes. If anyone dared to suggest a different approach or delay a minute longer in getting that diaper changed, they would get their heads chewed off. And by anyone, I mean my husband.

In addition to the stresses of being a rookie mom, I decided to take on the role of entrepreneur. In my heart, I knew my children weren't suitable for daycare, so staying home with them while running my own business felt right for me. Yet, the self-doubt I had as a new mom only grew stronger when I decided to become a new business owner.

I questioned everything, both as a mom and as an entrepreneur. Within the first year of motherhood, friends, family, and even strangers, weighed in on how I was raising my child. What supported me the most during that first year was the bonding time I had with my son. It helped me nurture my own intuition and learn how to read my baby's energy.

I found the same in business. Everywhere I went, someone had an opinion about what I should be doing and how it should be done. I sacrificed sleep to follow step by step of proven strategies. Being a new mompreneur left me fatigued.

It was challenging to find joy in the moment. I would be holding my sweet baby, but my mind was constantly stressing about money and scrutinizing my business. My business was literally being squeezed with a tight grip around its neck. I felt desperate for my business to work so that I could financially add to my family's well-being while staying at home with my baby.

My desperation led me to seek help. And as the saying goes, when the student is ready, the right teacher shows up. One day, while working with my baby boy playing next to me, I met my mentor in a Facebook Group. She helped me to see how my energy affects every aspect of my life. How it impacted how I played in my business and how I showed up for my children and family. Learning about my energy changed everything within a week.

When I said yes to investing in myself further with my mentor, I signed two private clients. She has shown me the importance of mothering myself and nurturing my soul by being clear about my desires, priorities, boundaries and, most of all, by owning my value.

And this is what valuing myself as a mom, wife, and entrepreneur looks like:

- I let go of guilt around household chores that I couldn't get to each day and I hired a house cleaner to support me and my family's needs.
- I addressed old conditioning from my childhood and generations of women before me.
- I brought focus to what I needed and I stopped comparing myself to other moms.
- I released the notion that I'm not fit or good enough as a mom.
- I brought awareness to my children and started to see them as their own person with their own thoughts, needs, wants, approaches, languages, and preferences.
- I started recognizing where I am not listening to myself.
- I created a boundary for myself to recognize the difference between running myself ragged and creating room both physically and emotionally to breathe and thrive.
- I started giving myself more time to accomplish tasks and I let go of the need to prove myself.
- I learned how to connect to my intuition and universal flow and creativity to support myself as a businesswoman.
- And I learned how to manage my energy and tune into love and creativity more often.

These adjustments in my everyday perception changed every aspect of my life. When I finally learned how to be in the moment, I let go of striving to be the perfect mom and loosened my grip on my business by addressing what I need first. Being present and standing in my personal power gave me the ability to align with what I wanted from moment to moment.

And there was never a more perfect time to be in the moment than during potty training. I've been a full-time stay-at-home mom for the last four years. I've supported both my sons during their potty-training days. There were days lost on the washroom floor waiting for my son to use the restroom. And during those hours, I was reminded that the only person I truly have control over is myself.

When I look within, my external world changes to my favor. Essentially, managing my own energy is at the core of manifesting. My desires are supported when I express myself as love, take aligned actions with clear intentions, and detach from the outcome with deep trust in the universe to deliver. Expressing myself as a loving woman often comes across after I would sit and pay attention to someone else's perception. So, while waiting for one of my sons to use the potty during potty training, I would stop and wonder what his perception was like.

He was so little. And up until that moment, all he knew was a diaper. Suddenly, that's gone and he's sitting on this huge, cold, hard surface. Maybe he worried he'd fall into it. He could have felt threatened or even worried about what would happen if he went potty.

My patience and empathy were tested. As was my confidence. I compared myself to other moms in my situation. I judged myself as a mom and worried others would look down upon me if my child wasn't potty trained by a certain age.

There was a big story in my head. My mentor helped me to get clear on my priorities. And then options became clear. He will always come first, and if that means to stay home another year then so be it. That could be a way to nurture my respect for him as his own person and be of support to him. This is the power of perception and trusting that whatever happens is for our highest good. All I can do is take aligned actions in going through potty training and be the best support in communicating with my son. Love him no matter what happens. In the end, my guy was potty trained after 3 days. The first day of school was rocky, we were called to pick him up after 10 minutes of drop-off. And he said he loves school on day 3.

Perception is everything. Time and time again as a mother, my lesson is love. It always comes back to love, which always sets me free to clearly see what's in front of me. Love nurtures my soul to thrive in every aspect: physically, emotionally, and spiritually. I remembered a slew of fear showed up when we first learned my son was diagnosed with autism. I worried about how others would see him with this label and how he would measure up with other kids the same age. I worried that his lack of social ability would impact his confidence and self-esteem.

I quickly learned to remember that he doesn't need to comply or conform to any societal standards. And it's been quite beautiful to uncover how he thinks and learns differently and to see him blossom even with the stigma that comes with his disorder. One night at dinner my younger one tried to get under his skin by claiming that he's the oldest. My son, at 5 years old, stood up and walked over to stand beside my little guy and said, "You see! You don't measure up." He is taller in height and it was the best way to show their age difference.

The most important role of a mother is to see both my sons for who they are—pure love and perfection.

Motherhood is a gift in perspective of the purest of hearts and love from our children. Also, my experience as a mom has been a privilege to have the opportunity to nurture my growth as well as influence the world.

I've witnessed innate wisdom from my children. Their open minds and souls have helped me access infinite time and space where magic lives. Being a mom of two kids, I've learned how to shift my perception with the snap of my fingers. Like magic, by staying aligned with their openness, I've learned how to tap into abundance all around me.

About Whitney Mullings

Whitney Mullings, a soul brand shaman. Her company works with transformational leaders using ancient shamanic techniques to show you how to pull your message from the heart, align your brand with purpose, and create a brand essence matching your vibration. Whitney loves giving leaders tools to stand out in a crowded marketplace while effortlessly standing in their value. Motherhood propelled her to be the leader of her life created a business and brand on purpose. Before that, she had over a decade of experience in marketing and communication in the fortune 500 company in Canada.

Whitney has been featured in The Huffington Post, Elephant Journal, and invited by Forbes as part of their coach's council covering topics on personal branding. Her two sons keep her on her toes. They are also her teachers on integrating the roles of a full-time mom and business owner can be easy and without sacrifices. Download her Personal Soul Brand Workbook (whitneymullings.com/pbw). Become a magnet attracting soul clients when the value of you is in the resonance of who you are as a brand.

You're Worthy of Everything You Ever Dreamed of

by Cara Wray

I'M WORTHY OF EVERYTHING I'VE EVER DREAMED OF!
At what moment in our lives do we start to look at ourselves and think this? That we're worthy of all the things we've ever dreamed of? At what moment do we look at the woman staring back at us in the mirror and say, "I love you, so damn much"? If you don't already feel this way, I hope that after reading this, your answer will be "today!"

I'm going to get very real with you. Let me take you back a few short years—2017 to be exact. It's the year my daughter was born. When I think back to the woman I was back then, I can't help but feel so much gratitude for my daughter. I wish I could go back in time and tell her everything was going to be alright.

In 2017, I was on the road to becoming a new mother. I was in a relationship with my now-husband, and he had two children from his previous marriage. He also worked away from home. I was learning how to navigate my new normal and I kept feeling as though I needed to please everyone or it would all falter.

I learned a lot of things about that woman. Things that have shaped me into the woman I am today. Back then, I never took care of myself on a personal level. I'm not talking about bubble baths and girl's night-outs, I'm talking about the real, raw and emotional healing that I seemed to avoid. I took such little care of myself and so much of others because, for some reason, I believed that everyone else came first. Everyone else's needs were to be met before my own. How ass-backward is that? To be honest, this is a societal belief that has been instilled in mothers for generations. And for far too long, it is one we have continued to believe is true.

Well, it's time for us to break the cycle.

It's time for us to dive into a "taboo" topic. Postpartum Depression and Anxiety. It's a very real experience that, when or if it rears its ugly head, I want you to know that this too shall pass.

Postpartum Depression and Anxiety affects 1 in 7 mothers. I was that 1. Postpartum hit me like a ton of bricks. They don't really explain it to you; the full-body experience and, as some may put it, the out of body experience you feel when you give birth to your child. And they sure as heck don't explain what happens after you give birth. So to the mama who is currently struggling, please know that I see you! But most of all, I've been you!

I remember the pain, nausea, confusion, fear, frustration, and the lack of support. I remember constantly feeling rushed, feeling angry, and feeling as though that was not the experience I had dreamed of.

I remember the many opinions of others during a very vulnerable time in my life. People telling me that I should have a natural birth and asking me if I was going to vaccinate my child. I was asked why I would choose to have an epidural, and whether I preferred a male or female doctor. I was told that I had to breastfeed because "breast is best" and that if I didn't, I would become a disappointment. I was told that my unborn child was disgusting because she was conceived outside of marriage. I was told that I wasn't trying hard enough. I was told not to eat so much, and then I was told not to worry because breastfeeding would lighten the load. The list was endless. I'm going to say this once … hear me loud and clear.

Be mindful of your words. What a new mother needs is support and to be heard. She does not need you to tell her what you think she should or shouldn't do!

There needs to be a discussion around the topic of self-care—ensuring that a mother is taking care of herself. There is a healing time. A time to be loved by herself beyond measure. A time where support does not need to be asked for. A time when a woman should never be made to feel guilty about her emotions and the overwhelm that comes with motherhood and the lists of should do's or could do's.

I remember coming home with our newborn baby and my first thought being, "boy, my house is a mess, guess it's time to start doing all the things." I remember feeling so scared of what might happen to our little girl. I was terrified. I was also in an immense amount of pain. I didn't fully realize what had just happened to my body and it was all happening so fast.

I woke up each morning, thinking to myself, "You can do it. Don't worry. You'll be fine. Your kids will be fine. I'll sleep later." This version of the woman I used to be was unrecognizable. I felt like a shadow of myself. I started picking apart every piece of who I was. I started worrying about my daughter's hiccups, the soap stain on the bathroom floor, my mind just would not stop. The worrying would not stop. The anxiety was crippling at times. To the point where I wouldn't do something because I was afraid of what the outcome would be.

As the sleepless nights continued, I felt immense sadness and frustration. This was an entirely new level of exhaustion; one I didn't want to become friends with. I felt trapped and more and more exhausted as the days went on. With the sleepless nights, the morning routines, the worrying, the doing, and the not doing, the guilt and frustration started to build upon itself.

I remember it like it was yesterday; feeling like I'd been hit by a ton of bricks. Feeling rage and frustration that I could no longer control. Feeling a deep sadness that rippled throughout my entire body. After more and more screaming day in and day out, with little to no sleep and the constant exhaustion, I had had enough! I remember snapping and screaming at my tiny 3-week old baby. I screamed and hollered for her to stop crying. I felt broken. I felt lost. I felt exhausted and I felt as though I had failed again because I couldn't soothe her. When it hit me what I had done, I fell to my knees in tears. I couldn't believe that I had just screamed at someone so small and so innocent. I didn't understand what was happening to me.

This happened in the same week that I was no longer able to breastfeed. My supply had simply vanished. Overnight. This added to my own disappointment. I felt as though my body had completely failed me.

The next morning, while sitting in the doctor's office with a hat covering my eyes, I asked for help. It was in that moment of complete vulnerability that I felt compassion for the first time from my physician. I felt seen. I felt heard. At that moment, I felt like I wasn't alone. My physician explained to me how very common what I was experiencing was. Then he asked me his first question: "What are you doing for yourself? How are you taking care of you?" I responded that I wasn't doing either because I didn't have the time. He responded by telling me that my "self-care is extremely important." Then he encouraged me to ask for help. He encouraged me to speak to someone about the behaviors that were presenting themselves. He made all my worries in one moment fade into a belief that everything was going to get better.

My physician placed me on medication to help manage how I was feeling. If you need additional help, please ask, there is no shame in needing help and asking for it. That stigma also needs to end, but that's a chapter for another day.

Self-care as a woman, and a mother, has been brushed to the side. We have been made to feel as though our wants, needs, and desires are less important than those of our families and it's truly time that we rise together and take a stance.

My story is much deeper; however, I believe that what I have shared with you will still have an impact. What I want to share with you is what happened after my experience and what has supported me through the birth of my second child. I believe and know this to be true because I fully embody my self-prioritization. And my hope is that you will too

Self-prioritization is "doing the first or important things first that matters to you the most." Meaning, you!

You come first. You lead! Always.

I want you to know:

It's okay to cry,

It's okay to ask for help,

It's okay to feel everything you feel.

You become stronger for it.

One day, when your littles become adults and experience the world first-hand, they will thank you for leading them with integrity, love, and grace. They will thank you for the lessons you taught them. They will thank you for leading them and believing in them. Most of all, they will thank you for taking care of yourself!

You are here to create the life you desire and to act towards bringing that life into fruition. Yes, even throughout motherhood.

You are here to lead.

You are here to pave the way.

You are here to shake things up.

You are here to set new standards.

I remember making the choice to put myself first. My peace of mind comes first. My dreams, goals, and desires come first. You have the power to make that same choice. I believe in giving my children the best possible life, but it will not be at the sacrifice of my own self-worth.

Your self-worth and self-prioritization come first. Always take care of yourself. You'll thank yourself for it.

To help you get started, I would like to share 5 Self-Prioritization tips with you that I have found useful over the years:

Acknowledge the emotions you're feeling. No longer suppress your emotions. Your emotions are valid. They always have been. The first step is awareness and acknowledgment. "What we focus on expands, and while that is true to a certain degree, what we ignore does not shrink, either!"

You know! You know what you need. You know what you desire. You know when a need of yours is not being met. Trust yourself. Tune into yourself.

Practice daily gratitude. Being grateful for everything that you have. I encourage you to have a separate journal that is filled with your daily gratitude. This is something you can look at a year later and truly anchor in just how amazing your life truly is.

Give yourself forgiveness for what you didn't know before. (Write yourself a letter of forgiveness.)

Give yourself permission to treat and place yourself as a priority! You matter. You have always mattered and you deserve to be loved by you. Always.

From one mama to another, I believe in you. You are doing amazing things in this world. You are seen, you are heard, you are understood. You are not alone. Together we rise. It starts with you.

You lead yourself. Always.

xo - Cara Wray

About Cara Wray

Cara Wray is a Mindset & Relationship Coach working with Mothers to nurture the relationships between themselves, their spouse and their children. She is also the founder of the Facebook community, The Sacred Mama Co., host of The Sacred Mama Podcast, a proud entrepreneur, wife, and mother/stepmother to four beautiful children. Believing that your strongest beliefs become your reality and together we RISE!

From India to Canada: An Intergenerational Journey of Courage, Action, and Meaning

by Vindy Teja

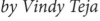

"**W**HY DIDN'T YOU TELL ME THAT PART OF THE STORY about Bibi before?! Like ten years ago? Or maybe even five years ago?" I exclaimed to my mother, the goosebumps clearly visible on my forearms.

Bibi, pronounced "Bib-ee" is a polite term in Hindi, Urdu, and Punjabi that's often used to address one's grandmother or an elderly related woman. My Bibi was my late maternal grandma. I didn't even learn her actual name, Raminder, until I was in my teens.

Growing up, Bibi was my confidante and roommate. As a direct result of the latter, I discovered she was also a snorer extraordinaire. I successfully categorized her snores into thirteen distinct sounds, an early sign of my organizing and structured thinking tendencies. When she was deep in slumber, I'd just have to nudge her a bit with my hand, and like a radio responding to a station change, she'd emit "The Whistle", "The Bear", or from time to time, "The Squeaky Wheel". In the mornings, I'd tease her endlessly, and she'd deny it all but her eyes would twinkle with knowing laughter.

"Well, why would I tell you that story," my mother replied in her native Northern Indian language of Punjabi, which she'd brought with her to Vancouver, Canada in 1968, along with her two-year-old firstborn son. Inderjit, my mother, was joining my father, Karan, who had set up shop in Canada two years earlier and was now legally entitled to sponsor his family.

Like immigrants from around the world who had been welcomed into Canada, my father and mother had dreams of living in a safe and democratic society, one that held the promise of greater security and independence—educationally, economically and socially—than would have been possible in India. Unbeknownst to them, they chose one of the most beautiful cities in the entire world, flanked by vast mountains and the Pacific Ocean, not to mention the mildest climate in the entire country. I never bought a real winter parka until my twenties, when I moved across the country to attend law school in Ontario. It was a rude weather awakening, that's for sure.

"It's such a sad and negative story," continued my conflict-avoidant mother. "I didn't see the point in sharing it with you and your brothers." This story – my mother's as much as my grandmother's – took place in a different time, culture, and country. But the parallels to my own story, which took place sixty years later during my early thirties in Canada, were undeniable. Parts of the story had filtered down over the years to me and my brothers, mostly due to my unending curiosity and relentless questioning. However, I realized us kids had just heard the PG version.

"But mom ... it explains so much about your feelings and your wisdom during and after my separation and divorce," I said, this time in English because I didn't want to risk mis-translating any words.

"Do you have any idea how important this story actually is?" I finally asked, quite bluntly. My obvious overemphasis of words in this conversation piqued my mom's interest, and she wanted to see where I was headed. "Maybe not, but I have a feeling you're going to tell me," she said, smiling.

My mom had just finished telling me the extended version of Bibi's involuntary marital separation from her husband—my maternal grandfather—in the 1940s, at a time when separation and divorce had not been introduced into Indian law. No for-mal legal rights existed to protect affected parties, especially women and children. If marriages did end, it was because the husband or wife had died. Separations no doubt occurred, especially if the conditions of marriage had become so intol-erable due to severe physical abuse of the wife. Unfortunately, in such a patriarchal society, many didn't even end then.

But my grandfather had been universally described by his family—and my grandmother's—as a respectful, intelligent and thoughtful man. Was this because I had the abbreviated PG story version? Or was there something more to it?

I already knew my maternal grandfather had been a Brig-adier General in the Indian Army in those days. He was sta-tioned at a base about a half day's journey away from the village he'd grown up in, where his wife, daughter, and extended family lived at that time. My grandfather would visit every month or two when he had time off work. As a teen, I remem-ber my grandmother recounting those family visits with such fondness.

At the time, India was still a British colony, so its army served under the British Army as part of the Allied Forces during the Second World War. My grandfather was deployed to Holland during the war when my mother was just a toddler. There ... he fell in love with my step-grandmother, a Dutch woman who was herself a widow with a young daughter. Needless to say, this complicated matters considerably.

After the Allied Forces defeated the Axis Powers in 1945, which included Hitler's Nazi Germany, my grandfather returned home. Before returning, he had written an impassioned letter to my grandmother, confessing his genuine love to my step-grandmother, and apologizing for the situation he had created. Bibi and my grandfather had had a traditional arranged marriage, and the first time they met was the actual day of the wedding, as was customary at the time. It was a "learn to love your partner kinda relationship", not a "fall in love with your partner kinda relationship". Though they had little in common other than their language, culture, and religion, my grandfather had shown his wife considerable respect while they had been together.

He implored Bibi, as well as his own family, to allow him to follow his heart and bring his beloved and her daughter to India so they could marry and start their life together. He promised to look after my grandmother and mother. He would send a monthly allowance from his army salary. He committed to educate and raise my mother together with his new family. He'd also give my grandmother his share of the family property if anything should happen to him. His family agreed and pressured my Bibi to do so as well. Bibi was in what seemed like an impossible situation at the time. She knew the balance of power and money was in her husband's and his family's favor. She worried about her daughter's future education and opportunities. She knew the quality of education my mother would receive in the village would pale in comparison to what she could receive if she lived with her father. She also had a lot of faith in my grandfather, who up to that point had been a man of his word. With a heavy heart, she agreed to go along with my grandfather's plan.

It's the next part of the story, which my mother had just finished telling me over tea in our brightly lit living room, which gave me those goosebumps and waves of serious reflection.

There was a legal impediment to my grandfather's plan. A major one. Although bigamy had not yet been outlawed in India at the time, it was specifically prohibited in the Indian Army. No exceptions. So if my grandfather wanted to remarry, he'd have to declare himself a widower, which he did. Turns out he told his Dutch beloved that he had been a widower with a small daughter, too.

"What?" I said to my mom. "He didn't tell his Dutch wife that Bibi was alive?"

"Nope," my mom replied. I let my mom continue the story. I was dying to find out what happened next.

True to his word, my grandfather sent for my mom and enrolled her in a good school. But then the instability that came with India's much-anticipated independence from Britain in 1947, demanded my grandfather's return to active duty. He'd be far away from my mom and his new family. He knew he could die. The reports of violence during the transition were well-known, and he wasn't confident that his new wife could raise my mother properly if something happened to him, so he had my mom safely transported to her own mother.

My grandfather survived the bloodshed that followed the 1947 Partition, but unfortunately, he never returned to get my mother. So my mother was enrolled in the village school and did a couple of years of college, the equivalent to a Grade 10 Canadian education. He did, however, continue to send the monthly allowance to his family, sixty percent of which was reserved for my Bibi. But a few years later, my Bibi's mother-in-law stopped giving her that money, claiming she didn't need it because she was living in her husband's home and didn't pay the household expenses.

That's when my Bibi realized it may have been wiser to take a stand right in the beginning, and not allow herself to be recorded as deceased just so her husband could remarry. She knew things could get worse for her, and especially for her daughter. Although my grandfather's land had been promised to my Bibi, her name was not actually on the title because she was "deceased" after all. It was her mother-in-law who held the Power of Attorney for her son and, judging by the allowance cut-off, there was no telling what else she would do to dishonor the commitments my grandfather had made.

My Bibi, a kind, uneducated and co-operative woman, stepped into courage and action. And she enlisted help. Her father and uncle accompanied her to my grandfather's home, a two-day journey by train. She had never been this far away from home in her life. When asked by the servant what her relation to the Brigadier General was, she replied: "I'm his wife!" She had lost her fear. She had nothing to lose. She had the primal power of a mother protecting her young. My grandfather's Dutch wife received a shock to her system, and quickly rushed to her husband's army office and brought him home.

My grandfather demanded to know why my Bibi had come to his house. They went out to his car to talk. Negotiation 101. No resolution. Bibi's dad and uncle stayed on the sidelines as back up, and Bibi soldiered on with the negotiations, without success. Bibi left his home, and I suspect my grandfather thought that was the end of it.

The same day, with no warning to my grandfather, Bibi took her dad and uncle with her to my grandfather's office and told his superiors that she was his wife and that he was not a widower. Well, that sent my grandfather scrambling. His employer was going to fire him, and his position and security with the army would soon be going up like a puff of smoke. He agreed to reinstate Bibi's allowance, not just the sixty percent, but the whole amount. And it would come directly to her, not to her mother-in-law. Luckily, Bibi's uncle knew the Defense Minister serving at the time. A phone call was made. My grandfather's position was saved.

Bibi went back to her home in her husband's village and raised her daughter with greater strength, grace, and security ... and a whole lot of love.

Although the circumstances of my separation were very different from my Bibi's, and hers took place at a time and in a country with many more patriarchal customs and few legal protections for women and children, I was still struck by the parallels ... and was determined to do something about it.

After a fifteen-year relationship, ten of which were spent in marriage, and one toddler later, I had been blindsided by my husband's announcement of our separation. Like my Bibi, the initial "shock and daze stage" led me to make decisions in the name of co-operation and family, that could have seriously compromised my financial position had it not been for the early support I had enlisted from friends, family, and divorce professionals. My Bibi eventually sought help from her family, but the cultural norms, as well as the pressure from her in-laws and husband, precluded her from doing it earlier when it could have helped her the most.

In my case, the long, stressful, and expensive divorce changed the entire trajectory of my life. Like my Bibi, it empowered and focused me as a parent and, like her, I found the courage to act and move forward, and not get stuck in anger and disillusionment. Eventually, I was motivated to integrate all my healing and learning with my legal training by adding divorce coaching to my professional coaching practice. I now had a real opportunity to help others make healthy decisions for themselves and their families during separation, divorce and life's many transitions.

After my mom shared the Mature Audiences version of Bibi's journey, I was able to see something else we had in common. Agreements around care and finances were actually discussed and made, and ultimately not honored without resorting to more extreme measures. My grandmother could not resort to the legal system at the time, but I did. This required considerable energy and resources, and I couldn't help but feel there had to be better ways to not only decrease divorce stress and costs but ways to foster communication and strengthen relationships from the get-go. So I decided to apply for and do a TEDx Talk, aptly titled "With This Prenup, I Thee Wed: The Truth About Prenups."

One of the parallels that struck me the hardest, and made those goosebumps jump out on my arms, was my mother's childhood pain of seeing her mother go through what she did, and of not having her father as a force in her life. She was two years old when it all happened, the same age my daughter was when I became separated. I empathized with my mother because my experience took her to a place in her psyche where she had probably not visited for decades. And I'm sure it was very painful.

The healing and happiness journeys are not simple, but I've realized that there are hacks that help us all get there. When I considered my experiences as well as those of my grandmother and mother, not to mention that of my clients, friends, family, and daughter … I couldn't help but notice how many of the same issues we all grapple with. I really wanted to find a meaningful and productive way to share ideas, strategies and real-life solutions with more people, so they could build happy lives from the get-go!

I followed this passion and wrote my book *YOLO: Essential Life Hacks for Happiness*. Of course, it is dedicated in part to my beloved Bibi, my confidante, and my roommate throughout my youth.

About Vindy Teja

Vindy Teja is no stranger to hacking her way back to happiness. She is a proud single parent, TEDx Speaker, Professional Life & Divorce Coach, and Author of *YOLO: Essential Life Hacks for Happiness*. She is a graduate of The University of British Columbia and Western Law School, and following her call to the B.C. bar, she discovered her coaching passion as Career Development Director at Western Law School. Along with many joys and successes, she's dealt with serious setbacks, personal and career challenges, not to mention pesky self-doubts. Her book, *YOLO*, dives into deconstructing happiness. Motivated by a strong belief that what doesn't kill you makes you stronger and funnier and that happiness is not a restricted club, she's distilled her results into practical and meaningful happiness life hacks in *YOLO*. Vindy's diverse background, including her own experience of divorce and parenting, has also equipped her with a wide lens with which to assist her clients and a continuing passion to serve others. She is an enthusiastic mom of an engaging teen daughter, who inspires her to be her true and best self every day.

Being a Mom

by Holly Hammerquist

THROUGHOUT LIFE, WE SEE ALL TYPES OF MOMS. AND, OF course, as women so often do we compare and judge them. Some moms looked well put together but were a mess behind closed doors. Some were the life of the party but weren't able to show up for their families the next day. Some moms looked tired but were exhausted because they did everything for everyone else. Some moms wanted everything to be perfect for every occasion but didn't let their kids lick the spoon after making cookies. Some moms were so uptight that the pillows in the family room couldn't be moved. We compare and judge moms without knowing their story. It's human nature.

Growing up, my mom was amazing and still is a rock star. She allowed her family to see who she really was as a mom. I saw the extremely hardworking mother who did everything for everyone else in the house. The mother who let us lick the spoon all the time because she wanted our holidays to be wonderful and memorable. I saw the exhausted woman after a long day and I saw the life of the party mom who deserved to cut loose occasionally. I also saw the mom who needed to sleep in after that party but still showed up to be with her family. I saw the mom who taught me how important it is to discipline your children in church and make them pay attention. I saw the mom who made it to every recital, game, and performance no matter how she was feeling. From watching my mother closely for thirty-four years, I was able to see that she was the most real, imperfect, wonderful teacher I could learn from.

Fast forward from childhood to twenty-nine years old and pregnant for the first time. I felt so many emotions from, "Oh crap, now what do I do?" to "I can't wait to snuggle my baby!" I remember thinking I was going to be one of those fabulous pregnant women you see in movies, or like the skinny girl next door who looks amazing while pregnant. I even thought I was going to read every pregnancy book I could find so I would be prepared for my baby's arrival. Well, that didn't happen! I was pregnant around the same time as a few of my coworkers and, of course, they felt amazing, hardly gained weight, didn't have morning sickness, and had zero complications. I, on the other hand, was sick, had gained a lot of weight, had gestational diabetes and high blood pressure. I read Baby 411, What to Expect When You're Expecting, and Pregnancy 411. Those books helped with maybe fifty percent of what I really needed to know. No one told me about the emotional and mental feelings that came along with pregnancy. Or everyone knew about those feelings but didn't want to say them out loud for fear of being judged by other women.

I remember the guilt I felt when I got mad at myself for gaining so much weight. I felt ashamed for my baby. There were times when I felt I had already failed as a mom because I wasn't pregnant and pretty. I was self-conscious and compared my pregnancy to my friends' pregnancies. Big mistake! But, of course, I didn't know that at the time. No one tells you this stuff. The moment people know that you're pregnant, women are going to give you advice whether you want it or not. And in all the advice I received, no one told me, "don't compare yourself to other moms!"

I can't really put into words the feeling I had when my son was born, but I'll try my best. I remember looking at him and thinking, "he's finally here, in my arms, and I created him." With help from my amazing husband of course. I remember how anxious I would get if I wasn't holding him or by him. I remember my heart racing because I wasn't in control of anything in my life. I had a hard time adjusting to my home life because suddenly, I remembered those "perfect" moms from my youth and the moms I had seen as an adult. They had done everything right in my view. Was I capable of being half as good as them? My baby needs to be on a schedule, my house needs to be spotless when visitors come over, I need to be washed and clothed. I remember seeing the worried faces of some of my family members because I was a little out of control about not being in control anymore. I felt guilty that I didn't have my shit together when I had always been the person who had her shit together.

That's when I realized how much those books about pregnancy had left out. They had left out the part about how other moms compare themselves to each other and try to compete. My child had colic and was not a good sleeper during his first 10 months. He would cry just to cry and I had horrible anxiety from not having my baby on a schedule or being able to help him with his crying. So again, I felt the mom-shame. As soon as I would hear him cry my heart would race! "I don't know what I'm doing!" I would think to myself. I read all those books and they didn't help me with anything but feel guilty that I didn't learn anything. I used to think that God prepared me for someone else's baby. I was not ready for my little guy. However, in the years of being his mother, I have learned more about myself and being a mom than I ever could have from a book. I learned that it's okay to not have it all together, to not be in control of everything, and I learned to roll with the punches. I also learned that God's plan to bless me with my Oskar was the biggest blessing of all. God wanted me to learn that I don't have to be in control of everything. But, of course, I didn't realize these lessons right away. It took a couple of months and a few struggles to see the horizon.

When I found out that I couldn't breastfeed my son, I felt awful and ashamed for my child. My breast milk literally didn't come in after giving birth. I'm the only woman that I know of who could grab her breasts and slap them around without any pain. No milk, just fatty boobs! The reason my milk didn't come in, was because I was so anxious about not controlling how my baby was acting, and more focused on why I wasn't the perfect mother with the clean house and post-pregnancy body, (Or what I thought the perfect mother should look like.) I put so much pressure on myself that when I called my mom and sister to tell them that I made the decision to bottle feed my son, I cried uncontrollably. I shamed myself again for not being able to breastfeed my child. My mother breastfed me, why can't I do it? I'm supposed to be able to do it, damn it! But, calling my mom and hearing her say, "It's ok honey. You do what you need to do for your baby," made me feel so much better. To have that understanding from my own mom was the best anxiety pill in the world.

After having had some of the guilt lifted from my shoulders, I felt so much better. I was able to relax and not stress about one more thing in my new-mom life. One of my best friends came over just to sit with me and the baby and ended up giving me some awesome advice. She said, "It's ok if the dishes don't get done. You and baby are more important." Finally, some guilt-free advice! It's ok if the dishes don't get done! Meaning, your house does not need to be perfect currently. Take care of yourself and the baby. It's so simple, but when you're stressing about everything, something so simple can be a lifesaver. My husband went out to Costco that night and got paper plates and cutlery for the next month. I know it's horrible for the environment, but for my sanity, it was worth it. It's ok if your house is not perfect, make sure you are taking care of yourself and your child.

Now, after about a month of not knowing what the hell I was doing as a new mom, I finally found my groove. Oskar was on a schedule to the best of our ability. I mean when I say this kid had colic, he had colic! So, we would listen to Creedence Clearwater Revival and Classic Rock all the time to soothe him. We'd go for walks, midnight car rides, swing time and warm tubby wraps to help him. My husband and I run shifts to stay up with him. I would have all day until 5:00 p.m. when my husband came home. Then he would take over from about 5:00 p.m. to midnight. Then I would take over again and, most of the time, Oskar would sleep for a few hours before starting the day again. But I remember this one night when my sleeping shift was done, I walked out of the guest room from upstairs and the song, I've Put a Spell On You by C.C.R was blaring throughout the house. I looked over the balcony and couldn't see my husband or son. I walked slowly into our bedroom and Brad was sprawled out on the bed and Oskar was laying down in the middle of the bed with a fence of pillows around him. All Brad could say was, "It's the only thing that keeps him calm." We found our sanity again! Another lesson not many people will tell you as a new mom is to do what you need to do to survive! If it's singing silly songs, 3:00 a.m. car rides, putting a vacuum under the kid's bed so they can listen to the white noise. Do it! The struggle is real, people!

Brad and I learned extremely quickly that it takes a village to raise a child, and we are very grateful to our family for supporting us, and to our friends for allowing us to vent and miss events during our adjustment period as new parents. Every day is a new challenge and you learn from it and keep on swimming like Dory. When Oskar was able to attend the school where I teach, it was a blessing and a curse. I was thrilled to be able to see him and hug him anytime I wanted to during the day. However, by being on campus I also heard from everyone about how badly behaved he was and how often he cried during the day. I had a really hard time adjusting again, this time to the new role of mom/teacher. I wanted so badly to disciple him at school, but then I would be stepping over the teacher's authority. I wanted to yell at him for acting the way he was but then I was embarrassed because I was a teacher and I couldn't even keep my kid in line. I always felt judged or looked at even if they weren't looking at me. Once again, the mom-shame feeling came back and stayed for a long time.

My school was amazing with our situation and we got Oskar some help with self-regulating techniques and that has helped us tremendously. I finally got over the mom's guilt that told me my child was not perfect and realized that I needed to do what I can for my son. To hell with the guilt, we worked with him so much to help make him feel successful and he is doing amazing. Oskar is an incredible little guy who surprises us all the time. I'm so happy that I learned to stop comparing my son to other children and not hide my head in the sand. We realized that he needed to work on some social/emotional techniques and we found a solution. Some advice I would tell new moms is to not compare your child with a sibling or with other children. Find out how your child operates. They don't come with manuals, so you need to use the trial and error method. I know it sucks and it will be hard. But if you don't put in the work with your child then they will continue to feel stressed and unloved.

I'm thirty-four years old now and pregnant with our second child. Our children will be about six years apart. I've had some questions of, "Why didn't you have them closer together?" I'll admit that again I felt ashamed for not trying for a second child sooner, but we weren't ready. My mindset was not ready. Also, God has a plan for you and I trusted in his plan for my family. He knew that I wasn't ready yet, and now I am. With this pregnancy, I feel more comfortable than the first time. I still have high blood pressure; however, I am learning how to control it with a low sodium diet and stressing out less. I'm not letting the fact that my house isn't always the cleanest, affect my state of mind this time. I'm saying, "no" to certain commitments for my health. I'm not comparing my pregnancy with that of my friends. I am comparing this pregnancy with my first because everything feels different on the inside and I feel like this baby is a girl. However, I don't know for sure yet. Of course, all we want is a healthy child. I'm proud of myself for how I'm tackling this pregnancy, which is another thing I've learned to do. To give myself credit where credit is due.

I know that I've shared a lot of personal information with you but, as I said before, you'll get advice, whether you like it or not. So, take this lesson from my experience and use it. Know that there are days when you will feel like you are the worst mother on earth. That you have failed miserably and you're the only one who's struggling. You're not a bad mom! You're imperfect, real, and the fact that you get up every day and try your best is amazing. Don't hide your struggle because you're afraid of being judged. Because, believe me, they're struggling too and could use some help, even if they don't say they're struggling. Share your stories with others so they can walk in your shoes and support you. Even if it's just a hug, it's not judgment. The struggle is real and women, in general, need to raise each other up instead of breaking others down. Remember you're perfectly imperfect and that's perfect for now.

About Holly Hammerquist

Holly Hammerquist, a wife, mother and teacher, has a bachelor's degree in elementary education and a masters degree in curriculum, assessment and instruction. Her hobbies are party planning, cooking and family game nights. She is currently pregnant with her second child and looking forward to expanding her family this summer.

The Great Legacy of Marriage and Motherhood

by Tara Severson

T HEY SAY THAT MOST PEOPLE, AT SOME POINT IN THEIR lives, want to know more about where they came from. For some, this leads to a search for biological parents. For others, this desire leads to a search for more information about their ancestors. There is a reason for the surges in ancestry websites and the uptick in DNA testing for family heritage. People search and begin to build those family trees, solid lines connecting Person A and Person B, from whom comes Person C. Sometimes Person C is famous, and people take pride in connecting those dots. Words like "once-removed" and "great-great-great" start being thrown around to establish those bonds. And if very lucky, some can form an impressive oak tree of lineage with a crown full of branches.

For a few, the desire for this family knowledge may have been cultivated from a young age. I was told about many branches of family relations, some trifling, at the knee, and for as far back as I can remember, my parents took me to all

93

the local cemeteries on Memorial Day for the tour of family graves. It was there that, perhaps a little ironically, the people in the stories often "came to life" for me because for the first time, while there, I saw their names in an existent, tangible way. I could touch the hard stone and poke my fingers into birth years and marriage dates, death, and epitaphs. Numerous memorials, especially on my dad's side, had epitaphs in German and I would insist that my dad translate them to me because I wanted to understand all that the tablets represented. I knew some of the many people my dad had known, such as when my own grandparents died and took their place among the garden of graves. Some were always and only known through the stories told, such as the infamous "Mutter" (mother)—a distant aunt of my dad who, I was told every year, "was not a nice lady." This perplexed and mesmerized me. Why would you give a term of endearment like "mother" to someone as unliked as her? Who decided to memorialize her in this way when the suggestion (I never heard the actual reason(s) for her "not nice"-ness) was that she was not a fondly remembered person? As fascinating as the mystery behind being unnamed and "not nice" was for me, I always felt a little sad for "Mutter." Imagine, I thought, people coming to your grave and remembering about you, first and foremost, that you were "not nice."

Fortunately, I come from and married into a great legacy of marriage and motherhood. Amongst my grandparents, parents, and my husband's grandparents and parents, there are over 320 years of marriage, thirty children, and fifty-one grandchildren. If I were to pursue the math to include uncles, aunts, cousins, and great-grandchildren, the numbers would continue to swell. And it isn't just a numbers game, though I think the numbers help tell the story. I have the great privilege of coming from great familial stability and security, love and nurture. Perfect? No. But is it the kind of bequest I hope to pass on to my own children? Absolutely. So, for their sakes, because that is ultimately what motherhood is about—doing things for the sake of the children—I thought I would record some of that legacy.

I keep my dad's mother, my grandma, tucked away in a little pocket in my heart. Part of this, I think, is because she never had the opportunity to meet my husband or any of my children, or to even see me grow up, as she fell asleep in Jesus when I was barely eleven years old. So, I often wish and wonder. I wish she could meet my husband (I know she'd love him!). Would she laugh at the funny things my children do? (Of course, she would. She had a gentle laugh and an established eye-twinkle that would appear at a great story). Would she be surprised at what I've become? (Yes, I think she would. This is the woman, the sainted woman, who never had an unkind word for anyone but once told my parents, "I think you might be in trouble with that one." I was that naughty as a young child). She was the story-keeper in the family, as well as the informal genealogist; she knew all the familial connections, remembered all birthdays, and retold all the stories. But the other reason she is so dear to my heart is that while she puzzled me as a child, she is also the one I most want to be like as a wife and mother. Steady and reliable, she led a simple life of quiet faith. She is honored amongst her children and was beloved by her husband. Wife of over fifty-five years and mother of five, she spent a lifetime beside her husband and nurtured her family. She did not have a career besides that of wife, and she did not have employment outside of being a mother. Upon her deathbed, she proclaimed to her family her confidence in the resurrection in Christ Jesus, and she expressed her desire to see each of her family members again. She maybe did not cut a wide swath of influence, but it sure ran deep.

My mother's mom, my grandma, is still with us. Some of my fondest memories with her consist of crossword puzzles, card games, and comic books. We both loved "Peanuts". She and my grandpa were married for over sixty-seven years and she too had five children. I had the great honor and privilege of telling her about my engagement to my husband, and later, the news that we were expecting each of my children. I used to call her on the phone and tell her stories of all the antics the kids were up to. When my husband was trying to convince me to get a dog, he elicited the aid of my grandma in an attempt to sway me. I remember, before my son was born, she was scheduled for heart surgery, and I told her, "Grandma, everything will come out all right. I will be there later this year to put another great-grandchild in your arms." I like to think that gave her some motivation in recovery. When she moved out of her home to an assisted-living apartment, I was shocked to find out that she had a box that held nearly every note that I had written to her over the years.

I always liked to hear the story of how my mom and dad met. They both worked at Green Giant one summer. My mom who was a nursing student at the time worked in the "first aid" department. My dad worked the lines, and my mom would often see him eating lunch during his break time. She kept telling a coworker, "I keep seeing this guy I want to meet." And the coworker kept telling my mom, "Well, I have someone I want you to meet." One day, my dad is said to have come into their work area and they all chatted for a while. When he left, my mom exclaimed to her co-worker, "That's the guy I've been wanting to meet!" The co-worker replied, "That's the guy I've been wanting you to meet!" Those were the first tiny steps that led to their marriage and, eventually, me.

My mother has a brother who is married but never had children. I remember my mom telling me often, "Not having children is a selfish thing." This was a hard thing for me to hear because, at that time, I thought I didn't want to have children. To be told by my mom that I was selfish was a terrifically difficult thing to hear, but she did not shy from telling me the hard truth. I appreciate that about my mom. Another thing I have always appreciated about my mom was her forthrightness in telling me my place as a child. She never withheld expressing her love to me, and she was always there for me (Who else would have suffered through all—and I mean all—those lousy elementary/middle/high school basketball games?), but it left me indignant to hear that my dad was the most important person in her life (after God, of course). When I married, though, I saw the goodness and rightness of that lesson and how important it is that that be true.

I also want to recognize my husband's side of the family because, without them, this would not be only half a family lore, it wouldn't be a story at all. Even at the time my husband and I first met, since one set of my grandparents was already gone, I appreciated and cherished the fact that I got to meet all his grandparents. And I couldn't be more blessed with my mother-in-law. I have much I could say about my love of and deep respect and gratefulness for, but I believe others are more qualified and better equipped to express that than I, so I will simply say that I am so honored to be a part of their family; I am so privileged, first of all, to be the benefactor of the wonderful son they molded, and to share in their heritage that is being passed to my children.

My own journey to motherhood perfectly portrays the adage, "When God hears your plans, He laughs." At the time I was entering college, I thought I would never marry. It wasn't any particular aversion, I just didn't have an interest in dating, so I thought that I wouldn't marry. I also thought that I would never have any kids. Conversations with my mom notwithstanding, I had not yet overcome my selfish desires. (And I still haven't. But kids help.) Kids were okay, but not something I needed to have hanging around all the time. And if by some off-chance, that I did marry and have kids, I decided that I would have all boys. Being a bit of a tomboy myself, I was pretty sure I wouldn't know how to handle a girl, so it would have to be boys. And, oh, yeah—I was not going to be a stay-at-home mom. I had better things to do. I had always been a good student, so I thought I would pursue graduate and post-graduate work. Whatever I did, I would definitely have a career. I'm sure you can guess where this is going. I was engaged a little after twenty and married two weeks after I turned twenty-two. I had my first daughter at twenty-three, and four daughters followed. Then I had my son. I have been a stay-at-home mom for the better part of sixteen years, and I still have years to go. But I would not change a thing. Yes, God heard my plans, and He laughed extra hard.

Sometimes, when I reflect back on my life as a mother, I'm dismayed: what kind of negative baggage will my children carry from my own failings and shortcomings? Where have I failed them? (I've already told them to change whatever they earnestly despise about my parenting … they just don't have to tell me—or announce it to my grandchildren). But I can also overestimate my negative influence and underestimate all the good that preceded me. When I remember this, I realize that ultimately, the future will be fun to behold. No matter how small the bricks I am contributing to the foundation-building, my children have a bedrock, built by so many others, to grow on. I often engage in "what-ifs" with my husband. (I'm not sure what he thinks of the exercise. I think it gives him palpitations sometimes). For example, if our eldest follows in our footsteps, marrying and having children at an age comparable to when we did, we could be grandparents in seven short years! If each of our children has even four children, we could have twenty-four grandchildren! And if each of their children has four children … Imagine!

The influence doesn't have to be that overt or sweeping to have meaning though. For as long as they can remember, I have made my children's birthday cakes. Every child got a chocolate cake to celebrate their first birthday, and at some point, they started choosing their preferences for the next year's cake. A couple of years ago, my eldest daughter asked me if, when she married, I'd be willing to make her wedding cake. When I said yes, of course, my other daughters asked for the same. Now, whether or not that actually happens, it touched me profoundly that they valued this small thing that I've done for them, so much so, that they wanted me to continue it to what will be one of the most important days of their lives. If it is truly their wish, I intend to give them that gift.

Upon reflecting on the legacy of all who came before me, I am now conscious of the fact that I am—and each of us is—but a quaking leaf on the stately oak of family. Take my dad's mother, for instance. She has been in the company of the heavenly hosts for, in our time, nearly thirty years. I am nearly the youngest grandchild on my dad's side, which means that, in, say, forty years or so, all living memory of my grandmother will be swept from this earth. (Now, I firmly believe with her that she lives with her Redeemer in heaven and will rise up in glory upon the second coming of our Lord, but that is the heavenly reality. I mean to talk about the earthly one). Another forty years or so after that, and the same will be said of me: anyone who knew me will too be in the grave. This is a deeply humbling realization, and, without the hope of the resurrection, it is a deeply depressing one. That leaves me with the final gift that has been handed down, and that, Lord willing, will remain with each of my children. That deposit of the faith. As valuable as everything else is, as precious as those legacies are, they are only worthwhile within the framework of Christ. I see a near-perfect illustration of that handing down of faith in my children's baptismal garments. Each of my children were baptized in the same gown that their great-grandmother, grandma, father, and aunts were baptized in. What a legacy. What a gift. That my forebears knew the gift they had—faith in Christ—and had the wisdom to pass it down ... truly priceless.

C.S. Lewis once said, "True humility is not thinking less of yourself; it is thinking of yourself less." As I try to live out this example given to me by so many faithful mothers, for my own children, I am thankful that I am able to, as the adage says, "stand on the shoulders of giants." And I truly do "stand on the shoulders of giants." That makes my own job so much easier, knowing that I am but a piece of my children's formation. Many other hands did the work first. So, while I can take this opportunity now to thank some of them (thank you!), I cannot thank them all right now. I can only pray for the day, in hope and expectation, when I will have that chance. And I will have that chance.

About Tara Severson

Tara Severson is a wife, mother to six, teacher, baker, athlete, volunteer, dog-walker and above all else, a Christian. She loves to bake, read, write and makes her health a priority. As a mother to five girls and one boy, Tara has learned how to juggle all her responsibilities. She is a champion for her family and passes down lessons of patience, acceptance, faith and values to her children.

Written by Carrie Severson, Tara's sister-in-law and publisher.

My Mother
Delilah Tintis Keenan

by Teresa Severson

I'M STARTING THIS STORY WITH A LITTLE BIT OF PLAGIARISM. I'm sure Mom probably would not approve. However, I'm going to go ahead and take a quote from the eulogy my brother gave at her funeral mass, in front of a full congregation at the Catholic church:

> "Delilah Keenan was a gem. A gem in so many ways.
> She was a believer. She believed in God and she believed
> in her faith when the load was heavy."

And that is very true. My mother was a gem of a teacher. She believed everyone should have the chance of a good education. She was the first woman in her family to go to college and always wanted to become a teacher. In 1940, she received her two-year degree.

She was married to my father for 59 years. She believed in the sacrament of marriage, in good times and in bad, for better or worse. If my dad were alive today, I'm sure he would agree she was a gem of a wife. She believed in Dad.

I was the youngest of seven children. When I was around 5 years old, Mom went back to college to earn her four-year teaching degree. It was not easy for her to be a mother of seven children to undertake this task, but she loved learning and sharing what she learned. This is why after earning her teaching degree, she taught in an elementary school for 35 years.

She believed in her children and reserved time for each of us, giving us individual love and attention. To say she was a gem of a mother would be an understatement!

Mom was a gem of a teacher, wife, mother, grandmother.

Mom was a believer in her faith, husband, children, and grandchildren

Now the brilliant light from that gem is shining on. She passed it on in so many ways and to so many others.

Mom, you were the perfect gem. I miss you every day and still feel you close.

About Teresa Deverson

Teresa is the mother of Carrie Severson, the publisher, Holly Hammerquist, an author and mother, and the mother-in-law of Tara Severson, an author and mother. She's a gem of a mother, mother-in-law, wife and grandma and we're all blessed with the lessons she learned from her mother. Teresa is the secret ingredient that keeps our village running. Thank you, mom for participating in this.

Written by Carrie Severson.

Color Me Beautiful

by Rachel Dumke

NOTES OF INCENSE MELDED WITH LYRICS OF "BE NOT Afraid", wafted out of St. Bernadette's ornate mahogany doors onto Harrison Street, beckoning summer breezes to "come follow me" and comfort the believers inside. A petite woman, a size two at best and no more than five foot three, with hand-crafted, rose-colored paper flowers pinned to her long blonde hair, sat tall and proud in a coveted pew near the propped side-door where the air wasn't quite so thick. Her fingers were firmly entwined with those of her floral artist, mine.

According to my skewed grade-school understanding of magnetism, I was north and she was south. Polar opposites, we would typically repel, but not on that day—at that moment, anyway. Mom lovingly said I was born with a pissed off look on my face and the reason we were so often at odds was not that we were opposites; rather, we were the same. I didn't try to understand her thinking. It was as puzzling as when I'd ask for a snack. She would give me an apple. If I refused it she'd say I wasn't hungry, I was just bored. When I wanted to pause at will and explore new things, she was always in a hurry. Even in prayer, her eyes were never at rest, always scanning child one, two (whose hand she was holding) and three. Fondly known as Moana, Groana, and Edwina, she was in disbelief that despite the heat, on that day, we weren't bickering. Her still cute swollen belly contained what would be her only boy, child four of what would someday be the "Ojala Six-Pack", but for now we all still fit across one pew. Perfect moments like these were relished. I imagine Dad who kept us contained by his post on the opposite end of the pew might have been smiling, at that moment, anyway. Given mass took approximately an eternity, he knew the peace was brief; mischief always ensued.

I wasn't the biggest fan of Sunday mornings as a child. Like every parishioner, my thumbs were drawn to the bubbles of cool metal that beckoned to be pressed, opening wide the jaws of each hat clip within reach, like a game of Hungry, Hungry Hippos. To avoid being the responsible party of the inevitable, accidental "thwack", I made the not-so-good choice to find a sibling to pick at. My butt was swiftly relocated, planted between the isle and my Mom's seat. Still in good spirits, I childishly played along with the day's "set-list" (which so far were proving to be my all-time favorite hymns) by flicking her long fingernails to the beat. I tried to busy myself in this way because if my behavior warranted it, I would be allowed to roller skate with neighborhood friends after mass on "the smooth part" at the end of the street. Dante and Danielle lived on the corner. Their house was a go-to destination because the village of Oak Park repaved their sidewalk with buttery concrete! From my front porch, I stood watch, riding my unicycle from banister to banister just like mom had me do when I, a ballet drop-out, was first learning to ride at age six. With each failed attempt, I checked off a box on graph paper, intent to prove her theory that I would learn before I filled up the sheet, wrong. I don't recall being right and she rubbed it in by having me apply the same method when learning new tricks. So on that day, two years later at age eight, I comfortably and swiftly paced atop one wheel impatiently waiting for my skate partners to return from their church.

The two always had vivid stories to tell about watching loose beads swirl around the brims of women's hats as they joined the congregation singing and dancing on pews. I opened their eyes to the injustice that in those same hours they were having fun, I endured torturous monotony; "Really," I said wide-eyed, "we just sit, kneel and stand." Horrified, they invited me to join their church and avoid such persecution. When the bulb horn blew for dinner I ran home and blurted out the details of their worship. "Can you believe the Spirit drew them to their feet?" I gasped in disbelief, "And they said we can go there, too!" In retrospect, I may have overstated my misfortune a bit.

Scripture readings sent my mind wondering and wandering, but it was far from the horrific image I left in the minds of other kids on the block. In fact, during the drudgery of the school week, I would sometimes sneak back into those same mental spaces and places. I wonder if my mother knew that as I felt the subtle ridges of her long natural nails, I was engrossed in imagining the largest and grandest of circus spectacles never to be seen. This private display was my hideaway where I processed the present and practiced being who I wanted to be. Dreaming unknowingly prepared me for a not-so-distant future that was not-so-out-of-reach. Here is what it may have looked like on that day when the faithful among me heard my music play ...

The first to move in time with my beat, I plucked from their seat to serve as the honorary band director who brought that Sunday's "Sanctuary Circus" to life. The choir transformed into an "Electric Company" marching band with uniforms of red and gold that sent waves of energy through my palms down to the soles of my feet. It shook the floor and every audience member rose from their seat. Each instrument emanated colors that aligned with their sound. Scanning the late morning crowd of worshipers, their attire determined their fate. Those who wore neon rolled down the side aisles on skates to platforms that rose up on either side. Partners spun and turned into one, a towering blur like stained glass windows of ultra-bright 80's light. Those in like colors became an act, tumblers in blues, jugglers in greens, tight-rope walkers wore pastel hues. My teacher, Mrs. Kerns' loudly patterned head-scarf and oversized vest became an ornate headdress and boa which proudly led a parade of pachyderms down the center aisle. Any classmate who wronged a peer that week would be cleaning up after them. Amy, my secret nemesis ever since Kindergarten when she knocked down my cardboard brick wall, was now in third grade and a perpetual part of this lower caste. Her overalls became unassuming gray coveralls which, too exhausted to change, she slept in, on a 70's sun-bleached, frayed-web, aluminum-tube reclining lawn chair just under the animal trailer in the corner of the backyard. In the humidity, it screamed as hideously under the slightest shifting of a human's weight, as the animal rights protestors did as they blew their hot air into megaphones, publicly shaming those who would come to see my show. God-fearing, they stayed outside, humbled by the heft and height of the magnificent church doors which pointed toward the heavens where, given their visceral hatred and spewing of venom, I knew they would never be. The doors closed like gentle giants, silencing the activists' outcries from the ears of the peaceable artists ready to take the center ring.

This now adult mind of mine has assumed artistic license to embellish the details of this purgatory of sorts that I placed those I disliked in so that it is as vivid and malleable as the production itself. To my credit, there was a way out—no show hand could stay heartless after spending time with such beloved creatures and their caring trainers. It took great compassion to allow someone I did not care much for near the animals I found so dear. Manual labor and animal therapy was my make-believe version of hope to erase the dark side of humanity (aka grade school bullies). The circus had the power to mold them, just as it did me in the ten years I performed in the ring with various shows from age eight through eighteen and a spattering of years beyond. Those real-life experiences added immense detail to my circus spectacular and would not have been possible without selfless parenting.

Flat-out busy, Mom always snuck in customized life-teachings for her six exceptional beings. She knew just the right time to do it too. Without fail, my single show each week was interrupted by communion, right when I had my patrons at the edge of their seats. Going with the flow, I broke for intermission releasing guests to the midway where my performers also served as ticket sellers and butchers selling novelties. Attendance at 9:00 a.m. mass was light so I utilized my small ensemble efficiently. Itchy feet ensued and I would begin to fidget if too much time was spent in reality. To help pass the time, Mom had me look at every person in prayer passing by on the return to their seat and say to myself, "The body of Christ." I found her request absurd, but I obeyed. Like most moms, she was clairvoyant and would know if I didn't. She had an honorary lifetime grandstand circus seat in my show, but I made a mental note to extend her an offer to be the feature Fortune Teller side-show attraction, offering priceless glimpses into luminous futures. I would have to, of course, bump the "Elastic Lady"—she wouldn't be happy.

Her assignment to me was humbling. After comparing notes as adults, I learned it was curiously given to only one other sibling. Some people made the words gush out of me, like babies of course, and the elderly. Kind-hearted, there were still a few towards whom I would mentally mumble. Each word was a heavyweight I bore as guilt for not truly believing—like the girl in my class who bullied one of my best friends out of school. You know her; the one in bull hand purgatory. There have been times when I couldn't see past the ugliness of human behavior. Anger would fester, get the best of me, and I couldn't bring myself to think "The body of Christ" at all. With age comes wisdom, and my flawed self is now far more and at times, too forgiving. For the most part, however, those four words brought my head out of the clouds and planted me firmly on solid ground. Fully present, I was alert, self-aware and stronger knowing my maturity was growing faster than it otherwise would. With continued maternal coaching, I began looking people in the eyes. In those exchanges I felt strangely exposed but with it came a surge of joyful energy. I realized our bodies are merely shells that house the true being. Never comfortable with the outside of me, I found some peace with an evolving theory that my soul was interconnected with those surrounding me. I created countless positive, micro-defining moments this way. Each connection I made added another Pantone strand to a three-dimensional web that had no beginning and has no end. When this exercise was applied outside of Church, I realized color can dissipate. Darkness exists and there are people and places your mind clearly states, "Turn around. Do not stay." Gut warnings take root as foreboding shadows of black and white; you choose the next move: fight or flight. There are a few memories I wish I could do over that perpetually replay. My quiet advocate, Mom encouraged my creativity and inspired me to see in color but she did not hide life's gray. Despite errors in judgment, I learned to trust my gut, and own the consequences when I didn't. Some lessons were serious, but others I learned in a humorous way.

I associated transformative people and events with precise colors. Each human, much like the instruments in my imaginary circus band, cast their own hue. My mom was special though, she had two—dusty rose and sky blue. In 1982, I immersed myself in the circus arts. Unicycling was my forte, and with strategically delivered encouragement from my Mom and circus family to try something new I slowly expanded my repertoire of skills with the Windy City Circus. The ring was the one place I found where you can be different and also fit in. It was quite a universe I got to live in. One of my first extended trips was to the Illinois State Fair. I was enamored with the beaded and feathered accessories adorning fairgoers' hair and hats. I fell in love when I spotted one in the crowd full of plush light blue plumes. I pursued every vendor on the grounds in pursuit of that one, as well as the perfect color for every other member of my family. I turned to the coin-pusher carnival games to grow my pot of (food) money (my parents gave me) which was being reallocated to roach clip souvenirs. I experienced the powerful addiction of gambling and the pain of loss—literally. Money tapped, I pretended I wasn't hungry until I was directly questioned by another performer, "When was the last time you've eaten?" I am sure Mom knew the story, but she never spoke about it and let it be my lesson on the importance of budgeting and vendor negotiations. No gift to my Mom since has produced a bigger smile, and I beamed as Mom clipped hers to her billowing bedroom curtains by her vanity—and the room was color-washed in a summery watercolor blue.

My skill set grew to the point that I was hirable on the circus circuit. Most summers and (extended) winter breaks were spent as a unicyclist and/or aerialist on the various collegiate and single to three-ring shows. Whenever possible, I assisted other acts or sold tickets for extra cash, my "cherry pie". I lived out of a suitcase. Each evening, we'd jump to the next town and explore our accommodations—typically a church, town hall or other public space. Years later, I upgraded to the back of a converted box truck. The people I met were as humble as the housing. The vast majority were genuinely good, but I often referred to the lessons Mom taught me in reading people and trusting my instinct. Though I was never homesick, if I saw a colorful object that made me think of someone, I was mentally equipped to budget accordingly, buy, and gift it to express they were loved and missed. I think with each sibling's birth, my independence exponentially grew. My parents taught me that sacrifice is required in the pursuit of dreams. Mine led me away from home. A parent now myself, I intimately understand how difficult that would be to let your child go and grow. I wrote letters to thank them and instill belief through my words that I was emotionally and mentally equipped enough.

The circus abruptly folded for me in reality. I tried awhile to sustain it, but through college, I planted seeds to vastly different but no less beautiful dreams. That said, I didn't always live life vividly and I know there were times I paled in comparison to the person I could be. Sluggish spots occur on every life course. I forgot in those times what the circus consistently brought out in me. Along the way, I would and still do revisit my imaginary production, and I play. Those who have impacted me earned permanent positions in my cast. It helps me process the present and is an exercise in future planning. There are unexpected cameo appearances in the show from those who briefly come to mind from my past, some who have passed and others ever-present who continue to grace my life. Amy, I learned, has traveled beyond this earth. She sometimes hangs around awhile and pauses awhile to observe it—modest herself, she stays in "the blues" which compliment her new hue.

Now older, shorter and blonde hair with roots somewhat gray, Mom interrupts me on the phone consumed in her own thoughts, talking as she feverishly digs through her same vanity for my paper creations she wore on her head, and that, "best gift ever, the clippy-thing with the sky blue feathers". I resign myself to listening and stare at the time-worn circus music box that Santa gave me with the dancing clown on the unicycle perched on my jewelry box. My mind drifts; I wonder what is in the single drawer, I forgot. She tells stories of my past that could not possibly be of me and of the future she envisioned that did not come to be. My life is better than that; I am sure she would agree. The topic turns to colors and how they still hold real value to me. She recognizes that and asks what color I saw in me. I didn't. It wasn't about me, you see. She tells me to look in the mirror. I always hated that but she poses the idea that perhaps the colors I saw in others, were a reflection of the various pieces I let people see of the full spectrum of me.

About Rachel Dumke

Rachel Ojala Dumke first sat on a unicycle at the age of six and entered the competitive world of unicycling soon thereafter. She attended her first National Unicycle

Meet at the age of eight and at the age of twelve earned the 1987 World Unicycle Queen title at international competitions in Edogawa, Japan. She began performing with Chicago's Windy City Circus at age eight and the Triton Trouper Circus at age twelve. During those formative years, her repertoire of circus skills grew and she began entertaining audiences outside of "the ring". Highlights include performing on The Bozo Show and serving as an opening entertainer at Bruce Springsteen and the E Street Band's 1985 concert at Soldier Field. She completed two summer tours and one winter tour with The Circus Kingdom and concluded her formal circus career as an aerialist with The Flying Valentines. Life brought new adventures including college, marriage, motherhood, and new career and creative pursuits (including writing), but she never let go of the circus … Or perhaps the circus never let go of her. She explored the financial services industry for twenty-five years and found her niche in talent development, but something was missing. Her writing often included cotton candy, sequins, band music, and one-wheeled things, revealing the unsurprising answer. This "awakening" allowed her to see opportunities that were always there. Rachel is now also a circus arts instructor, helping youth shine brighter by providing a safe place for the exploration of self through the circus arts. Rachel lives in SE Wisconsin with her husband, who agreed to eat fire with her at their wedding, and their two boys.

Together Apart

by Nilda Campuzano

MY MOM IS NOT UNLIKE ANY OTHER MOTHER, AND SHE is not unlike any other mom who lives and raises children in poverty. Millions of mothers all over the world struggle from day to day to provide for their children, to protect them, to nurture them, and to bring them up with little comforts that they hope would someday make their children look back with fondness on their childhood memories.

Mothers are strong, courageous, resilient, managerial, and at times, simply magical in the way that they make something out of nothing. My mother was a master at the latter.

I grew up in a very small town in Mexico's Northeastern region. We lived a humble life growing up; money and resources were scarce, but Mother always found a way to make things work. She could create feasts out of minimal ingredients and, with the expertise of a magician, there was always enough food to feed 5 children and a husband. How she ever managed to do it is still a mystery to me. However, that is not something she learned when she married my dad. Before she even met him, my mom was already experienced in the art of making something out of nothing, in giving before expecting to receive, in putting others ahead of herself, and in never, ever giving up.

My mother was the fourth child in a family of eleven. As one of the oldest in her family, much of the workload involved in raising a family fell on her shoulders. The pictures of my mom as a young lady are very blurry, but her beauty defies black and white photographs. The way she stood, the way she smiled, the way she carried herself, tells the story of a woman who left a trail of pixie dust wherever she walked.

People who knew her then all speak of her breathtaking beauty, her disarming smile, her drive to succeed and her deep love for all. Her love was the sacrificial kind. It never mattered how tired she was or how little resources she had, she always made sure her parents and siblings had everything they needed. She left her home at an early age to go to school to become a seamstress; she moved away from her family and everything she knew, in hopes to better the financial well-being of her family. Her bravery and decisiveness are admired by many.

Her father was her rock; I could tell so by the way the tone of her voice changed when she spoke of him. Many of the lessons I grew up with were rooted in him, in his loyalty, his fierceness, his honesty, and his empathy. My mom takes after him. She lost him way too early in life, but she bravely steeled herself to live life without him, becoming the backbone of her family. By then, she had become a wife and a mother, and many of the hardships she faced at home carried over to her new life.

The workload resting upon her shoulders was crushing. Imagine raising a family without electricity or running water and all of the commodities those two items afford you. Laundry was done by hand, after spending a couple of hours walking back and forth fetching water at dusk, from the neighbor's house one block away. At the time, the small town we lived in was still developing; the electric and water service stopped one block away from our house. I recall a certain nostalgic feeling I felt looking at our neighbors' homes lit at night, while we sat by the dimmed light of an oil lamp.

Cooking was also a challenge for my mom; at certain periods of time cooking was done over a fire when, for one reason or another, we did not have a stove or gas to make the stove work.

I remember the physical effort she had to make to keep our family running, but I was too young to realize that we lived in poverty and that there was no end in sight. I couldn't fully grasp the concept of worry my mom must have felt, not knowing where our next meal would come from. I couldn't read her heartbreak to see us wearing old clothes and shoes and wishing she could give us more. I couldn't measure the depth of her frustration, not being able to give us the idyllic childhood every mom dreams of.

In addition to the demands of raising a family, my mom also played her role as a Pastor's wife. She married into a life of ministry and service to God and His church. My dad is approaching 53 years as an evangelical minister. I often wonder if she really knew what she was getting into when she said "yes" to dad's proposal. I can't help but wonder if the role took her by complete surprise. Either way, being a Pastor's wife meant she had two families to care for: her own family, and her spiritual family. And the demands of her spiritual family were perhaps greater than her own family's. Cleaning, doing laundry and feeding a family with very little resources pales in comparison to looking after the spiritual well-being of souls.

The rural area in which my father was a minister was uncharted territory. There were no protestant churches in the area at the time, and many new little settlements were popping up all over the place, surrounding the main town we lived in. My dad loves God and is passionate about His church, so his vision was to take the gospel to the whole region. They visited every single little town or settlement and started working with a family, investing time, effort and what little resources they had for a long time until that location grew enough to go from a church's mission to an established church. The churches my dad planted decades ago still stand and flourish to this day.

As rewarding as those decades were, they took a toll on our family, especially mom.

She became a workhorse that kept going, checking all the boxes: making sure food was on the table, laundry was done, children were on time to school, homework was done, good grades were achieved by all, all church services were attended, people were counseled, church activities were organized and seen to completion, the church building was cleaned up, fund-raising activities were promoted and executed, all the t's were crossed and all the i's were dotted. Like a little robot. Like the little engine that could, chugging up the mountain.

That's how I learned to be who I am today. It was an unspoken lesson; a lesson passed down by action, not by words. She simply didn't quit, she never stopped loving and she never held back from giving. I watched her tangibly be the glue that not only kept our family together but the church also. Little did I know that I was going to have to practice the lessons learned from her on strength, courage, and resilience so early on in life.

In my early twenties, my little world came crashing down after the sudden loss of a boy I loved; that loss introduced me to grief, and grief coupled with a streak of rebellion, set me up on a path I had not foreseen: I emigrated to the United States and started life from zero.

I worked hard, I hustled, I made sacrifices. Just like my mom. I moved on, strong and decisive. I stumbled, but I steadied myself; I fell down, but I got up again. I stared at the future unafraid. Just like Mom.

I was strolling through the park one summer day while listening to a very charismatic preacher talk about standing your ground and speaking truth against the battles we might be facing. Suddenly, and to my big surprise, I began to long for my mother; It had been 23 years since I left home, and even though we saw each other at least once a year, I grieved for all the mother-daughter things we never got to experience.

Due to the physical distance between us, my mother was not at my wedding, nor at the birth of either one of my three children; I missed having her near, being mothered by her as I was attempting to mother my own children. I missed being pampered by her during the hard days of childrearing, during those days when I was simply exhausted from the physical demands of the job. I missed crying to her when the little cracks in my marriage became insurmountable gaps; I missed her holding my hand when I walked out of the courthouse with a divorce settlement neatly tucked in my purse.

I was overcome by a sense of grief for all the years lost, for the missed opportunities, and the separation of our souls.

However, in the middle of that grief, I was comforted by the knowledge that in a very tangible way, I am just like my mom; I am fierce when it comes to making sure my family has everything they need, even if that means working two or three jobs. And just like my mom, I had to be strong, especially emotionally, in order to raise three boys in the post-divorce turmoil. I have this affinity for helping people, to sacrifice for them, to comfort them and nurture them with a million-dollar smile that brings life and hope to those on the receiving end, just like my mom.

That realization brought with it the assurance that despite the distance, Mom and I could never really be apart, because who we are, what we do, and how we love, keeps us united.

The biggest lesson I have learned from my mother is that you are who you are; and who you are must be embraced, celebrated, nurtured and protected. I have learned that I am one hundred percent qualified to be who I am, but I am completely unqualified to be someone else. I learned that God does not demand anything from us that does not bring us closer to Him through joy, peace, and love. I learned that spiritually taking care of others while our own spirit languishes is not a divine endeavor.

Above all, I have learned that despite all her failures, her disappointments, her frustrations, and her exhaustion, my mother carries inside of her a fire that cannot be quenched; that her love for God surpasses all of the material lack she experienced and that her message brings life, joy, and strength to those who are blessed to hear her speak.

That day, at the park, I was granted the grace to see my Mom for who she really is, and all I could really do was to humbly ask God for a double portion of all she is because, in a very real and tangible way, I want to be not just who she is, but also everything she didn't get the chance to be.

About Nilda Campuzano

Nilda's lifelong dream has been to write and speak, but she has kept all of that to herself after believing the lie that she did not have anything good to offer the world, and that her life experiences were something to hide, not publish. Those lies came crashing down when she met women who were boldly sharing their stories and setting others free by recounting not just their falls and failures, but their rise and their victories. Nilda is now boldly stepping out of her comfort zone and letting her breakdowns become her breakthroughs, one story at a time. Nilda believes that out of the abundance of the heart the mouth speaks, so you can follow her personal search for a healed heart in her private Facebook group W.a.S - Women and Swords; in it, she inspires women to grow in the understanding that our tongue is a double-edged sword that can bring either life or death into our life, and encourages them to speak life into every area of their life. Nilda resides in Pewaukee, WI with her three sons and a beautiful Native American Shepherd furbaby named Azula. You may contact Nilda by sending an email to justnilda@gmail.com

Don't Marry a Mexican

by Linda Rubio

A LESSON I LEARNED FROM MY MOTHER HAPPENED IN THE kitchen. I was 11 years old and she was hustling around the kitchen getting dinner ready. "Don't ever marry a Mexican!" she said, out of the blue. What followed was complete silence and no eye contact.

I remember hearing these words my entire life, and at times they were said so randomly out of nowhere. My initial defensive reaction was irrationally yelling, "I never even want to get married!" Then, of course, you couldn't deny that this was such a racist statement for her to say. In reality, that comment had nothing to do with race or even the act of getting married.

My mother was born and raised in Mexico. She grew up in a small ranch town in the middle of Mexico. In her teens, she was crowned as the town's first official Beauty Queen and always had a strong desire for more than the life she was born into. She knew that if she stayed, she would end up like everybody else. She would be married off young, have lots of kids, and then her kids would do the same. She dreamed of opportunity outside of her small town so, in her late teens, she embarked on a journey by herself to the land of the free. She crossed the border into the U.S. illegally, was homeless, and eventually made a life for herself. She even crossed the border illegally multiple times to bring other family members back to the U.S. for a chance at a better life.

Her first language was Spanish and mine was English. In fact, both my parents were from Mexico, they spoke Spanish to each other but only English to me.

My mother didn't want me to suffer because of my race. She wanted me to be accepted as an American and not get held back in Kindergarten for speaking Spanish. Unintentionally, it also created a barrier with our communication with each other because her English was broken.

The broken communication between my mother and I created walls and emotional distance.

In my teens, I created answers to all the questions I had about life and answered to no one in my family. All this without the internet! I was terrified all the time but refused to be vulnerable. I wanted so badly to hear some of her personal thoughts but, by now, I was not letting my wall down for anything or anyone. Even though I fought her on everything, I tried to tell my mom that I loved her, but I never did.

In my late teens, I moved out but kept a strong loyalty to my mom because I could never imagine my life without her. We were very cordial with each other except for the occasional disagreements I initiated. For the majority of the time, however, it was like nothing had ever happened. I knew she was always excited to see me and worried about me all the time. Her worry was made very clear to me, as well as her way of expressing her love for me.

In my early 20s, my mother ended up living with me. It was after the stroke that left her temporarily paralyzed. My father didn't want to take her to the hospital and, without any emotion, said: "she's old and old people are supposed to die." So with my sister's help, my mom moved in with us.

My mother's wounds ran very deep, causing her to become silent. She would eat and go to her room. She moved around slowly with her head down. She felt like a burden with no purpose to live. My mother was silenced by others and then she silenced herself. As much as I fought for my mom to speak up, I also learned to live in silence. My inner authority was collapsing by my mid-20s just as hers did. This left me feeling even more lost and insecure in all areas of my life. This is just one example of what generational trauma can look like.

The life my mother made for herself was not a luxurious one. She survived physically and barely mentally and emotionally. She never wanted to talk about what happened to her when she crossed the border into the United States. Even though she lived and carried that trauma, she was very spiritual and a healer with herbs and natural remedies. Her vegetable and flower gardens were vibrant and flourished in any environment. She spent joyful hours in her garden and that place gave her something nowhere else in the world could—peace. Today, I tell her grandchildren she was the OG (Original Gangster) of holistic living. She was an artist who painted beautiful paintings with deep, rich colors. She had a desire to be the best at whatever she did and she thrived and flourished in the kitchen.

Every meal was always fresh and served on a nice plate with a fancy glass. For breakfast, there was always fresh-squeezed orange juice. Smaller meals like sandwiches even tasted gourmet. And I could always sense a deep pain behind her eyes. Then again, there was a deep pain in every ethnic woman I saw growing up. It was normal for our women to suffer in silence. We had generations of wounded women helping wounded women.

It was rare for my mother to talk about her thoughts and feelings. She listened to others and helped everyone around her. And when things were painful at home, she would isolate herself in the bathroom. After cleaning the bathroom from top to bottom, she'd draw a bath and soak for hours.

Growing up, I heard, "Don't ever marry a Mexican" more times than I can count. Even though that statement was imprinted into my mind, I ended up having a family with a Mexican. Despite her warnings and years of witnessing her pain, I repeated a cycle. And I never grasped the full beauty of the meaning of that statement until I was on my knees begging God for help with my severe postpartum depression.

While my daughter was sleeping, I threw myself to my knees, shivering from the pain, and cried aloud to God for help. My body went numb and right before my eyes, I saw my mom's life.

My mom had been gone for a few years by the time I had my daughter. And yet, "Don't ever marry a Mexican" still ran so loud in my head.

I finally got it. What she had been trying to tell me for years had to do with my soul's desire and the fire burning deep within. She was trying to tell me to beware of the people I surround myself with and to be cautious of people in my life who will put out my fire.

We all have a fire burning deep within us. It lights up our world. It keeps us moving forward through life's challenges. It's in our eyes and people notice it without having to ask us about it. Women have a burning desire all our own and my mother was trying to warn me to guard mine since I was 11 years old.

My mom had a burning desire within her that only came alive around me and my sister or when she was uncovering her own spirituality.

That burning desire we all have leads us down our path to living our truth.

"Don't marry a Mexican," was my mom's way of describing what her soul was fighting for. She wanted her own life. It was not about a specific race or getting married. In her silence, she lost her ability to speak the truth of what was in her heart. My mother did her best to survive and express what she could. That statement encompassed all of her regrets; for letting her fire go out and not wanting me to do the same.

She was walking around in the dark, buried alive by all of her trauma, and struggling to figure out how to be a mom with no help. She lived with a fear of losing her kids, being homeless, standing up for herself, and following her dreams. She was not allowed to share her feelings and thoughts at home. A space that was supposed to be safe and non-judgemental. Home was a scary place for her. Not to mention all the unacknowledged passed-down generational trauma. She tried her whole life to conform. Purposely lost her indigenous identity so that her kids could thrive in the U.S. She slowly and painfully lost interest in everything and everyone. Eventually, she never picked up another paintbrush, cooked another delicious meal, held another fancy dinner party, dressed up in her stylish swag, walked on her own, or spoke another full sentence. She wanted to die, and she did. She died when she was wheelchair-bound at 63. She looked defeated and decades older.

After the night that I finally got my mom's lesson, my life changed.

My wish for death turned into a plan for rebirth. I needed someone who could help me through to the next stage of my life — recognizing this as a gift of self-evolution.

I knew if I could get through this unbearable stage of my life, I would also heal my mom's legacy. I started where my mom left off. I tirelessly searched for spiritual guidance and healing. I searched for every healing modality and therapeutic option possible. Now I had the internet, so I searched for other stories like mine but couldn't find any. It was a slow and painful process but what helped me to move forward were the rituals.

My mother had rituals and, even though she didn't talk about them, they were apparent. When the rituals stopped, any little bits of herself that she was hanging on to also vanished. At the time, I despised having to walk across rows of salt around the house and not being able to use the lemons that were designated for extracting negative energy. But when it all disappeared, I felt a sense of emptiness.

I was already overwhelmed with my role as a new mom. I needed to create rituals of my own that flowed smoothly without creating additional stress of having to do more. I sang the same heart to heart song every time I put my baby to sleep. I took photos of our hands growing older together every day. I talked to my mom every night after putting my daughter to bed. I sat under the full moon allowing her embrace to fill me with hope.

Simple, yet life-changing. Rituals created a sense of security in a time of such uncertainty. They were more than just daily things to check off my list. They were done with prayer and the intention of healing the pain. Months later, these rituals helped me to feel less guilty about the time I thought I had lost because of severe postpartum depression.

I was fueling my fire little by little even on days when I felt like I had no life left in me while functioning as a single mom. I still suffered heavily for almost a year but I was moving forward. We were no longer going to be silenced.

I carry the lesson behind that statement with a fierce conviction and continue to teach my daughter the same. My fire is sacred, and it is up to me to keep it burning. I have a responsibility to heal my wounds and heal from passed-down generational trauma. I am here to take up space and not to play small to make others feel comfortable or out of fear. I honor that I come from a family of women warriors, torch-bearers, here to light the way for future generations.

About Linda Rubio

Linda Vasquez Rubio is a mom, mentor, blogger, and author. She has spent years helping moms multiply the manifestation of their soul's work. She is guided by the Divine Mother energies of the cosmos to help create clarity so her clients can activate, embody, and surrender to their dreams. It is important to her legacy to help nurture the rebirth of her community to amplify the blessings poured on the planet. Find out more about Linda Vasquez Rubio at inspireandempowermoms.com/lindarubio.

Conclusion

Every mom has a lesson or two to share. And we're grateful to pass down a few lessons we've all learned along the way.
Love,
Mom